ROLES OF
THE ATTORNEY GENERAL
OF THE UNITED STATES

Luther A. Huston
Arthur Selwyn Miller
Samuel Krislov
Robert G. Dixon, Jr.

July, 1968

PUBLISHED AND DISTRIBUTED BY THE
AMERICAN ENTERPRISE INSTITUTE
FOR PUBLIC POLICY RESEARCH
WASHINGTON, D.C. 20036

© 1968 American Enterprise Institute for Public Policy Research, 1200 17th Street, N.W., Washington, D. C. 20036. All rights reserved under International and Pan-American Copyright Conventions.

Library of Congress Catalog No. 68-25123

Price: $2.00

THE AUTHORS

LUTHER A. HUSTON was Director of Public Information for the Department of Justice for four years under Attorney General William P. Rogers. For two decades, during the administrations of nine attorneys general, he covered the department and the Supreme Court of the United States as a correspondent in the Washington Bureau of *The New York Times*. His books include *Pathway to Judgment: A Study of Earl Warren,* and *The Department of Justice.* Mr. Huston is now Washington correspondent for *Editor and Publisher.*

ARTHUR SELWYN MILLER is Professor of Law in the National Law Center of The George Washington University. Previously he was Professor of Law and Editor of the *Journal of Public Law* at Emory University. Dr. Miller holds degrees from Willamette University (A.B.), Stanford (LL.B.), and Yale Law School (J.S.D.). He is author of numerous law journal articles and several books on constitutional and administrative law. His books include *The Supreme Court and American Capitalism,* and *Private Governments and the Constitution.*

SAMUEL KRISLOV, Professor of Political Science, University of Minnesota, was educated at New York University (B.A., M.A.) and at Princeton (Ph.D.). Before joining the faculty at the University of Minnesota, he taught at Michigan State and the University of Oklahoma. Dr. Krislov's contributions to various journals of law and political science include *The Amicus Curiae Brief* which appeared in the *Yale Law Journal* in 1963. His most recent book is *The Supreme Court and Political Freedom.*

ROBERT G. DIXON, JR., Professor of Law in the National Law Center of The George Washington University, formerly taught Political Science at Maryland, American, and Syracuse Universities. Dr. Dixon holds the A.B. and Ph.D. (political science) degrees from Syracuse, the J.D. from George Washington, and was a Ford Foundation Faculty Fellow at Stanford University. He has served as Chairman of the Committee on Supreme Court Decisions of the Association of American Law Schools, and is author of books and numerous articles. He is widely known for his writing and lectures on legislative reapportionment. Supported in part by grants from the Rockefeller Foundation and the American Philosophical Society his research in this field has culminated in his most recent book, *Democratic Representation: Reapportionment in Law and Politics* (Oxford University Press, 1968).

AMERICAN ENTERPRISE INSTITUTE
For Public Policy Research

THE AMERICAN ENTERPRISE INSTITUTE FOR PUBLIC POLICY RESEARCH, established in 1943, is a nonpartisan research and educational organization which studies national policy problems.

Institute publications take two major forms:

1. LEGISLATIVE AND SPECIAL ANALYSES—factual analyses of current legislative proposals and other public policy issues before the Congress prepared with the help of recognized experts in the academic world and in the fields of law and government. A typical analysis features: (1) pertinent background, (2) a digest of significant elements, and (3) a discussion, pro and con, of the issues. The reports reflect no policy position in favor of or against specific proposals.

2. LONG-RANGE STUDIES—basic studies of major national problems of significance for public policy. The Institute, with the counsel of its Advisory Board, utilizes the services of competent scholars, but the opinions expressed are those of the authors and represent no policy position on the part of the Institute.

ADVISORY BOARD

PAUL W. MCCRACKEN, *Chairman*
Edmund Ezra Day University Professor of
Business Administration, University of Michigan

KARL BRANDT
Professor of Economic Policy (Emeritus)
Stanford University

MILTON FRIEDMAN
Paul S. Russell Distinguished
  Service Professor of Economics
University of Chicago

GOTTFRIED HABERLER
Galen L. Stone Professor
  of International Trade
Harvard University

C. LOWELL HARRISS
Professor of Economics
Columbia University

LOY W. HENDERSON
Director, Center for Diplomacy
  and Foreign Policy
American University

FELIX MORLEY
Editor and Author

STANLEY PARRY
Professor of Political Science
Trinity College, D. C.

E. BLYTHE STASON
Dean Emeritus, Law School
University of Michigan

GEORGE E. TAYLOR
Director, Far Eastern &
  Russian Institute
University of Washington

OFFICERS

Chairman
CARL N. JACOBS

Vice Chairmen
HENRY T. BODMAN
CLYDE T. FOSTER
H. C. LUMB

President
WILLIAM J. BAROODY

Treasurer
HENRY T. BODMAN

TRUSTEES

HENRY W. BALGOOYEN
HENRY T. BODMAN
JOHN M. BRILEY
FULLER E. CALLAWAY, JR.
WALLACE E. CAMPBELL
FREDERICK J. CLOSE
RICHARD J. FARRELL
CLYDE T. FOSTER
HARRY C. HAGERTY
WALTER HARNISCHFEGER
JOHN B. HOLLISTER
ROBERT A. HORNBY
EDWIN HYDE
CARL N. JACOBS
JAMES S. KEMPER, JR.
RAYMOND S. LIVINGSTONE

FRED F. LOOCK
H. C. LUMB
WILLIAM L. MCGRATH
GEORGE P. MACNICHOL, JR.
ALLEN D. MARSHALL
DON G. MITCHELL
CHARLES MOELLER, JR.
DILLARD MUNFORD
HARVEY PETERS
H. LADD PLUMLEY
EDMUND W. PUGH
PHILIP A. RAY
W. F. ROCKWELL, JR.
HERMAN J. SCHMIDT
WILLIAM T. TAYLOR
R. C. TYSON

THOMAS F. JOHNSON
Director of Research

JOSEPH G. BUTTS
Director of Legislative Analysis

EARL H. VOSS
Director of International Studies

CONTENTS

I. HISTORY OF THE OFFICE OF THE ATTORNEY GENERAL — 1
   Luther A. Huston

II. THE ATTORNEY GENERAL AS THE PRESIDENT'S LAWYER — 41
   Arthur Selwyn Miller

III. THE ROLE OF THE ATTORNEY GENERAL AS AMICUS CURIAE — 71
   Samuel Krislov

IV. THE ATTORNEY GENERAL AND CIVIL RIGHTS, 1870-1964 — 105
   Robert G. Dixon, Jr.

OTHER AEI PUBLICATIONS — 155

I.

HISTORY OF THE OFFICE OF THE ATTORNEY GENERAL

by Luther A. Huston

Origin and Early History

THE ATTORNEY GENERAL of the United States runs the largest law office in the world but he has only one client, the government of the United States. The basic function of the Department of Justice, of which the attorney general is the head, is to represent the interests of the United States in the courts. The attorney general is the government's law enforcement officer.

Since the Office of the Attorney General was established by the Congress in 1789, there have been 66 different attorneys general. Edmund Randolph of Virginia was the first; Ramsey Clark of Texas the sixty-sixth. One man, John Jordan Crittenden of Kentucky, served twice—once under Presidents William Henry Harrison and John Tyler, and nine years later under President Millard Fillmore. Orville H. Browning, also of Kentucky, served ad interim for several months in 1868 while also serving as secretary of the interior.

When Randolph became attorney general in 1789, the office could not have been smaller and scarcely more poorly paid. Randolph received $1,500 per year and had to pay his own rent, buy his own stamps and stationery, and furnish his own heat and light.

He had no assistant. He was not required to provide the government with a record of his work. In fact, when the ninth attorney general, William Wirt, took office in 1817 he was amazed to find no records to guide him in performing his duties. His predecessors had kept no books, no correspondence files, and no compilation of their official opinions. The first compilation of opinions was not published until 1840—a half-century after the office was created—and the records were still unsatisfactory when Homer Cummings became attorney general under President Franklin Roosevelt in 1933. Incomplete letterbooks, opinion books, and bales of manuscripts and correspondence covering the period from 1817 to 1870 were stored in the Library of Congress and huge masses of undigested papers accumulated during that 50-year period were in the none-too-orderly files of the Justice Department.

Today the Department of Justice has more than 32,000 employees and an annual budget of more than $400,000,000. The salary of the attorney general is $35,000 per year. The deputy attorney general, the solicitor general, and nine assistant attorneys general help him direct the work of the department. The director of the Federal Bureau of Investigation, the director of the Bureau of Prisons, the commissioner of immigration and naturalization, the pardon attorney, and the chairman of the Board of Parole are officials of the department under the attorney general's supervision, as are also the United States attorneys and United States marshals in the 92 judicial districts into which the country is divided.

The growth of the office of attorney general from a one-man shop into a vast and complex organization is an inseparable part of the story of the development of the United States and its institutions. Every attorney general from Randolph to Clark has participated in great events and crises and as the role of government has expanded, so has the role of the attorney general.

The common law of England has often been cited as the fountainhead of the American system of law and jurisprudence. The English system did provide guideposts for the development of legal institutions in this country and a system of law practice and enforcement existed in America during colonial times. But it was the injustices of the British system as applied to the colonies that the colonial leaders sought to correct and, when they set about establishing machinery for the enforcement of federal laws in the original 13 states, their objective was to protect the individual and political freedoms George the Third and his predecessors had trampled upon. Fearful of perpetuating in the New World the tyrannies of the Old, they were reluctant to create a strong central legal system. Consequently, they borrowed the title of attorney general from the English but, otherwise, the office as established and developed in the United States is in no way a facsimile of its British counterpart. It is, as Chief Justice Fred M. Vinson once said of the Supreme Court, "almost sui generis."

There were attorneys general, under that title or some other, in the colonies before the Revolutionary War. Richard Lee, for instance, was the first attorney general of Virginia, appointed in 1643, and in 1650 the General Court of Rhode Island appointed an attorney general and solicitor for that colony. In 1704 the Assembly of Connecticut directed the appointment in each county of "a sober, discrete and religious person . . . to prosecute and implead the laws."

"Three Masters"

It has been said that the attorney general has "three masters"— the President, the Congress, and the courts. Although the attorney general is responsible to the President in the exercise of his discretionary duties, his basic authority is derived from Congress and his functions are subject to congressional control. His powers, like the President's, "must stem either from an act of Congress or from the Constitution."[1] The Constitution does not mention an attorney general, and so, as pointed out by the Supreme Court,

> . . . the functions of the Department of Justice, the powers and duties of the Attorney General and the duties of his assistants, are all subject to regulation by congressional legislation, and . . . the department is maintained and its activities are carried on under such appropriations as in the judgment of Congress are needed from year to year.[2]

The attorney general, as required by law, makes an annual report to "the Senate and the House of Representatives of the United States in Congress assembled."[3]

---

[1] Youngstown Sheet & Tube Company v. Sawyer, 343 U.S. 587 (1952).
[2] McGraw v. Dougherty, 273 U.S. at 178.
[3] See *Annual Report of the Attorney General* for the fiscal year ending June 30, 1966.

In fact, in 1924 the Congress ordered certain cases taken from the attorney general and placed under the control of special counsel. The attorney general at that time was Harry M. Daugherty who later resigned as a result of a Senate investigation of his conduct.[4] In other cases, where there has been a conflict between the position of the President and the position of the Congress, the Congress has appointed its own special counsel.[5]

Many years ago (1887) the Supreme Court called attention to the fact that the Congress had provided "no very specific statement of the general duties of the attorney general," and that the question of his authority "is one surrounded by some embarrassment." [6] The Court has taken a broad view of the authority of the Department of Justice, but at the same time it has noted "the enormous power and its capacity for evil . . . reposed in that department."

The federal courts, of course, also have some control over the activities of the attorney general. Like all other members of the bar, he is in a sense "an officer of the court" and subject to the court's direction in certain respects insofar as litigation is concerned. As shown in Professor Krislov's paper (chapter III), the courts can— and do—call on the attorney general to act as amicus curiae or to aid them in the enforcement of their orders.

The Congress created the Office of the Attorney General in 1789 and it existed under that title until 1870 when it became the Department of Justice. The Judiciary Act of 1789 provided for the appointment of "a meet person, learned in the law, to act as Attorney General for the United States." It assigned to the attorney general the responsibility to "prosecute and conduct all suits in the Supreme Court in which the United States shall be concerned" and to give opinions on questions of law, when requested, to the President and heads of departments.

U.S. Attorneys and Marshals

The Judiciary Act perpetuated, in a different pattern, the system of county attorneys and deputy attorneys general of colonial times. Each United States attorney was to be "a meet person learned in the

---
[4] McGraw v. Daugherty, 273 U.S. at 151.
[5] See, for example, the case of Lovett et al., 328 U.S. 303.
[6] United States v. San Jacinto Tin Co., 125 U.S. at 278.

law to act as attorney for the United States" in the prosecution of "all delinquents for crimes and offenses cognizable under the authority of the United States, and all civil actions in which the United States shall be concerned."

The law enforcement machinery was further strengthened by a system of marshals, one in each district, to "execute all lawful precepts directed to him." These marshals, now 92 in number, have played an important role on occasions of domestic disturbances. Their broad authority to help preserve the regular processes of justice was affirmed in the famous 1890 case of *In re* Neagle, in which the Supreme Court said:

> . . . we hold it to be an incontrovertible principle that the government of the United States may, by physical force exercised through its official agents, execute upon every foot of American soil the powers and functions that belong to it.

Under the "lawful precepts" directed to them, marshals have been used to quell disorders in labor disputes, to put down Indian uprisings, to enforce court orders in racial segregation situations, and otherwise to keep the peace of the United States. In more routine duties they maintain order in courtrooms, serve subpoenas and other legal documents, guard federal juries, have custody of prisoners while in courtrooms, and arrest persons charged with crimes.

Part-Time Job Until 1853

Having created an Office of Attorney General and a rather embryonic system of law enforcement, Congress was apprehensive about the potential threat to state and individual rights and liberties, and so it was less than lavish in providing funds and personnel. It was not until nearly 30 years after the formation of the federal government that Congress reluctantly agreed to provide the attorney general with office space (in the Treasury Department), a $1,000-a-year clerk and a contingent fund of $500 a year to pay for stationery, stamps, fuel and a "boy to attend to menial duties."

George Washington was aware that the pay was low and the job might not be attractive to qualified appointees. When he asked Randolph, his aide-de-camp in war and his attorney in private life, to become the first attorney general he held out the bait that the office would "confer pre-eminence" upon the occupant and gain him a "decided preference of professional employment." In other words, Randolph could practice law privately and capitalize on the prestige of his office. He did, and so did his successors up to Caleb Cushing, the twenty-third attorney general. By 1853 when Cushing took office, the salary had been raised to $8,000 and the occupant did not have to pay the expenses of the office out of his salary.

Neither the Judiciary Act nor any other law required the attorney general to reside at the seat of government. Few of them did and the early attorneys general were likely to be in Washington only when Congress was in session or the Supreme Court was sitting—but even that was not obligatory. In 1814 President James Madison proposed legislation requiring the attorney general to "keep his office at the seat of government during the session of Congress" and William Pinkney, then Madison's attorney general, threatened to resign because of the residence requirement. Congress did not pass the law. Pinkney resigned for other reasons but Madison extracted from his successor, Richard Rush, a pledge to reside in Washington when Congress was in session. Cushing was the first attorney general to reside full time at the seat of government.

Services to the Congress

The law did not define the relationship of the attorney general to Congress. But, from the outset, Congress looked upon the attorney general as its lawyer and asked for opinions as to the drafting and constitutionality of legislative proposals. The attorney general thus became for Congress its principal authority on constitutional matters, although many lawyer legislators often disagreed with his interpretations. Giving opinions to the legislative branch became an increasingly heavy burden and in 1819 Attorney General William Wirt put a stop to it. Wirt held, in an elaborate paper for President James Monroe in which he outlined his conception of the functions and responsibilities of his office, that opinions had been given to Congress as a courtesy, not as a matter of law, and that if the practice was to continue, Congress should revise the law. In general, Wirt's successors adhered to his position. But in modern times Congress has obtained the views of the attorney general simply by asking him to testify on pending legislation within his jurisdiction. Congressional committees now employ their own legal staffs to advise them on matters of law, and the House and Senate each have an Office of Legislative Counsel staffed with a highly competent corps of lawyers.[7]

Rank of Attorney General

Although Congress created the executive departments, it did not specify who should, or should not, be members of the President's cabinet. In the early years the attorney general was not accorded cabinet rank but rather served as counsel to those who were. The first meetings of Washington's cabinet included only the secretaries of foreign affairs, war, and treasury. But Randolph was Washington's legal adviser and he began to attend cabinet sessions on March 31, 1792. Thus almost from the beginning, attorneys general have had a hand in making policy as well as interpreting and enforcing the laws.

Under an act passed in 1886 the attorney general ranked fourth in line of possible succession to the presidency. The bill provided that members of the cabinet should succeed in order of seniority and since the Office of Attorney General was the fourth created, the incumbent of the office held that rank. Later the line of succession was changed, but for protocol purposes, such as seating at the cabinet table, the attorney general still ranks fourth, after the secretaries of state, defense, and treasury.

Creation of the Department of Justice

The Department of Justice evolved slowly. Beginning with Randolph there were continuing proposals to enlarge the jurisdiction of the attorney general's office so as to give it control of all of the legal affairs of the government. On the other hand, at various times Congress assigned special legal functions to officials in other departments, for example, as in the 1820 act that created a solicitor of the treasury to direct all suits for the recovery of money or property of the United States. Recommendations by several early Presidents, particularly Andrew Jackson, that a "Department of Law" be created were rejected by Congress, although as early as 1830 the Office of the Attorney General was being referred to as the law department. A "Department of Justice" was first suggested in 1851 by Alexander H. H. Stuart, secretary of the newly-established Department of the

---

[7] Gerald D. Morgan, once Assistant Legislative Counsel on the House side, later served as Special Counsel, and Deputy Assistant, to President Eisenhower.

Interior. But no action was taken until February 25, 1870, when the Joint Committee on Retrenchments, a congressional committee appointed chiefly to find ways of reducing government expenditures, reported out a bill to create a Department of Justice. The bill was enacted into law four months later and the department officially came into existence on July 1, 1870. President Ulysses S. Grant named Amos T. Akerman of Georgia as the first attorney general to head the new department.

The law created only one new position in the department, that of the solicitor general of the United States. It provided for two assistant attorneys general, gave the attorney general complete direction and control of United States attorneys and all other counsel employed on behalf of the United States, and vested in him supervisory powers over the accounts of district attorneys, marshals, clerks, and other officers of the federal courts. It also greatly expanded the administrative duties of the office. The law made no change, however, in the duties of the attorney general with respect to giving official opinions and advice.

Present Organization and Operations

Personnel

The attorney general, of course, heads the department and "its functions are all to be exercised under his supervision and direction." [8]

The next ranking official is the deputy attorney general, who assists in the overall direction of the department and becomes acting attorney general when the head of the department is absent. The second ranking official is the solicitor general who is directly in charge of all government litigation in the Supreme Court and determines when appeals shall be taken in cases lost by the government in the lower courts, and when the department shall intercede in the role of amicus curiae.

In addition there are nine assistant attorneys general, each in charge of a division. The assistant attorney general in charge of the Office of Legal Counsel is chiefly responsible for preparing the formal opinions of the attorney general, giving informal opinions and legal advice to governmental agencies, and assisting the attorney general

---

[8] 273 U.S. 135, 150.

in performing his functions as legal adviser to the President and the cabinet. The administrative attorney general is often called the department's "housekeeper" since he is the business manager, prepares the budget, disburses and accounts for all expenditures, supervises the recruitment of personnel, purchases supplies and equipment, collects and compiles statistics, maintains and disposes of records, and directs the distribution of mail.

The duties of the other seven assistant attorneys general are more or less obvious from the titles of their divisions, which are Tax, Civil, Lands, Antitrust, Criminal, Civil Rights, and Internal Security. They are responsible for litigation in their various fields.

The attorney general may delegate to these assistants all questions of law, except constructions of the Constitution, and their opinions have the force and effect of opinions of the attorney general when endorsed by him.

Other operations under the attorney general are shown on the accompanying chart.

The FBI

In terms of both personnel and operational scope, the Federal Bureau of Investigation is the largest single unit under the direction of the attorney general. The FBI is the investigative arm of the department and the primary civilian intelligence agency of the nation. It employs more than 14,000 people at headquarters and in branch offices throughout the country. It may be called upon to investigate any apparent violation of federal law, and its highly trained agents go into the field in a variety of federal cases from kidnapping to stolen automobiles. In recent years, subversive activities, a growing criminal underworld, and the problems of civil rights have kept the FBI busy and in the limelight. It cooperates with, but does not supplant, other investigative and protective agencies of the government, such as the Secret Service, the Bureau of Narcotics, and the Central Intelligence Agency.

Prior to 1924 the FBI's operations were none too efficient. It had been created by Attorney General Wickersham in the administration of President Taft but had never been organized into a capable, smooth-working force. When Harlan Fiske Stone became attorney general in 1924 he reorganized the bureau and put J. Edgar Hoover, then a young lawyer, at its head. Hoover continues in office at this writing and has built the bureau into one of the world's most efficient crime-fighting forces.

Federal Prison System

The federal prison system was formally created in 1891. In that year Congress authorized the construction of three prisons but failed to appropriate money to purchase sites or erect buildings. Nothing further was done until 1895 when the military prison at Fort Leavenworth was transferred to the Department of Justice. That was the nucleus of a system that now includes nearly a dozen prisons, reformatories and correctional institutions with a population of more than 25,000 prisoners.

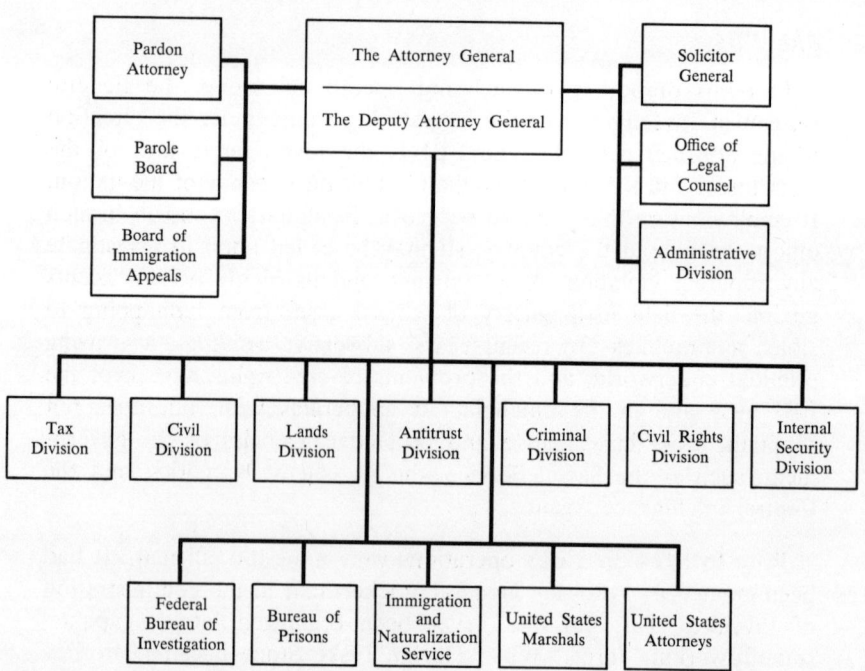

DEPARTMENT OF JUSTICE

Problems of Neutrality and War
Washington's Neutrality Proclamation

During Randolph's tenure as attorney general, the questions of neutrality and the rights of neutrals became an urgent problem. France was at war with England and the United States was bound to France by treaties of alliance, amity, and commerce. Pressed by France for assistance, President Washington refused to become "entangled." At his request, Randolph drafted a proposed proclamation stating that the United States would pursue an impartial course as regards belligerents, would refuse protection to American citizens engaging in hostilities or trafficking in contraband, and would prosecute those who violated the laws of nations. Washington made this the basis for a state paper issued April 22, 1793, which laid down the policy of neutrality that was a cornerstone of American foreign policy during many perilous times.

Subsequently, Charles Lee of Virginia, who also served Washington as attorney general, would have scuttled the neutrality policy. French authorities suggested to the American commissioners in Paris that certain controversies might be settled more in accordance with their government's wishes if it would bolster France's exchequer with $250,000. Lee was outraged and boldly proposed a declaration of war. He said a de facto state of war already existed—although there had been no formal declaration—and advocated an embargo on French ships, the opening of American ports to British privateers, the arming of American merchant ships and revocation of the exequaturs of French consuls. The President did not take his attorney general's advice.

Role During the Civil War

Because of the activities of some European countries in behalf of the Southern cause, neutrality problems arose during the Civil War. Legal questions on neutrality were largely overshadowed, however, by the internecine conflict, and the opinions and advice of attorneys general during that period related largely to specific incidents, such as smuggling and the seizure of blockade-running ships.

Espionage During World War I

Thomas Watt Gregory of Texas was President Wilson's wartime attorney general but there is scant evidence of his participation in great wartime decisions. After the declaration of war it became Gregory's obligation to deal with espionage. At the outset laws were lacking to cover many offenses and Gregory asked Congress to enact 17 new laws as weapons to combat the activities of spies and saboteurs. All but four were incorporated in the Espionage Act of June 15, 1917.

An interesting opinion by Attorney General Gregory, dated September 16, 1914, held that the President had authority to censor radio stations and to close down or take charge and operate stations that failed to obey the mandates of the neutrality proclamation of August 15, 1914.

Jackson's Ex Post Facto Opinion

Novel questions pertaining to the powers of the President were referred to the attorney general before and after United States entry into World War II. They arose, in the main, because of President Franklin D. Roosevelt's departures from traditional concepts and practices. One involved the new doctrine of lend-lease, a plan that contributed to Allied success in the war but aroused storms of controversy. *After* the President had negotiated an executive agreement with Britain to exchange 50 over-age destroyers and other obsolescent military equipment for certain off-shore naval and air bases in the Atlantic, he asked Attorney General Robert H. Jackson if the President had the authority to make such an agreement without Senate ratification. In an opinion dated August 27, 1940, Jackson advised the President that he had constitutional and statutory authority to carry out the transaction without submitting the agreement to the Senate. Whether Jackson was aware that some of the ships already were in British hands at the time was never officially disclosed.

Opinions of Attorney General Francis Biddle

Immediately after the attack on Pearl Harbor, Attorney General Biddle ordered the internment of German, Italian, and Japanese aliens in order to safeguard internal security and to prevent the aliens from committing crimes that might bring down harsh punishments. More dramatic, perhaps, was Biddle's participation in the trial of eight Nazi saboteurs who landed on the eastern coast in the summer of 1942, equipped with money and explosives to sabotage key industrial centers. Biddle held that they were triable by a military commission and successfully conducted the prosecution. When the Supreme Court was specially convened to hear a petition for habeas corpus, he again argued the case and habeas corpus was refused. Biddle's role in these two controversial incidents is treated more extensively in chapter II, "The Attorney General as the President's Lawyer."

Attorney General Tom Clark

Biddle's successor, Tom C. Clark, took office after World War II. He advised President Truman that the war powers of the President did not cease automatically with the end of actual fighting and he upheld, in an opinion on June 7, 1947, the power of the President to transfer to France certain ships captured from German and Japanese navies. Clark also advised President Truman that a presidential agreement under a joint resolution of Congress to permit establishment of United Nations headquarters in the United States had the same binding effect as a treaty.

Internal Security

Internal security became an acute and controversial issue after both world wars. Fears of anarchistic elements led to drastic measures after World War I and apprehension generated by the growth and zeal of communism led to restrictive legislation after World War II.

"Palmer Raids"

One of the most bizarre performances by any attorney general involved the so-called "Palmer raids" of 1919. A. Mitchell Palmer, a Pennsylvanian, was appointed attorney general by President Wilson on March 5, 1919. He had hardly settled in office when prominent persons throughout the country began receiving bombs, mostly through the mails. One was planted on Palmer's own front steps and blew the steps to bits. Public clamor ascribed the bombs to anarchist plots and demanded government action. Attorney General Palmer instructed William J. Flynn, former head of the Secret Service, to ferret out the anarchists. A General Intelligence Division, the forerunner of the FBI, was established within the Department of Justice and in less than four months it had indexed the histories of more than 60,000 persons—among them prominent teachers, writers, and clergymen—who allegedly were identified with radical movements or propaganda. Several bills introduced in Congress proposed various measures for suppressing peacetime sedition, but none passed. Palmer, however, acted. In a series of raids conducted under his direction more than 5,000 persons were taken into custody. American citizens were turned over to state and local authorities for prosecution; aliens were turned over to the Bureau of Immigration for deportation. The raids were widely denounced and there were relatively few prosecutions or deportations.

The Harding Administration, which followed Wilson, brought in Harlan F. Stone as attorney general. In 1924 he established the FBI and set new patterns of investigations. He specifically directed all investigators or agents of the Justice Department to confine their activities strictly to matters within the scope of their legal authority.

Anti-Communist Activities

The Communist party, after World War II, came to be regarded as the foremost domestic threat to national security. The attorney general's basic statutory weapons for dealing with the threat were (1) the Smith Act of 1940, which provided punishment for conspiracy to teach and advocate overthrow of the government by force and violence and made membership in an organization which so advocated a crime; (2) the Labor Management Relations Act of 1947, known as the Taft-Hartley Act, which required officers of labor unions desiring to use the services of the National Labor Relations Board to execute non-Communist affidavits; and (3) the Internal Security Act of 1950, which established the Internal Security Division in the Department of Justice, charged it with enforcing laws against espionage and subversive activities, and all laws relating to treason, and required all "Communist-action" and Communist-front" organizations to register with the attorney general. The Communist Control Act of 1954 and the Labor-Management Reporting and Disclosure Act of 1959 modified certain provisions of the above-mentioned laws but did not alter their main objectives. Enforcement of these laws placed a heavy work-load upon the Internal Security Division and the FBI.

Role of the Supreme Court

Beginning in 1949, more than 100 leaders of the Communist party were convicted under the conspiracy and membership provisions of the Smith Act. In 1957, the Supreme Court reversed most of these convictions, ordering new trials or acquittals. Prosecutions continued and more than 50 persons were convicted, of which 30 or more served prison sentences. Before the non-Communist oath provision of Taft-Hartley was repealed by the 1959 Disclosure Act, nine persons were convicted of conspiring to defraud the government by obtaining the services of the NLRB through the use of false affidavits.

Although the Subversive Activities Control Board three times found the Communist party to be a "Communist-action" organization, neither the party nor any member of it registered with the attorney general as required by the Smith Act. Instead, the party challenged the board's findings in the courts. In June, 1961, the Supreme Court affirmed the board's decision. The party was then indicted for failure to register and found guilty after a trial in United States district court. On December 17, 1963, the Federal Court of Appeals for the District of Columbia reversed the conviction, holding that to require officials of the party to register would deprive them of the Fifth Amendment protection against self-incrimination. The Supreme Court refused to review the case and thus left standing the appellate court's decision. At this writing the Justice Department had not decided what further steps it might take.

Prosecutions

During the 1950-60 decade 19 Soviet officials were asked to leave the country because of espionage and several Soviet citizens, lacking diplomatic immunity, were convicted and imprisoned. The source of much of the information involving Soviet agents and Americans was Elizabeth T. Bentley, who had engaged in Communist activities during World War II. In November, 1945, Miss Bentley disclosed to a Senate Judiciary Subcommittee the names of government employees she said were members of or giving aid to Soviet spy networks. As a result of her disclosures and subsequent Justice Department investigations, various individuals who were or had been in government service were convicted of contempt for refusing to answer questions of investigative bodies, or of giving perjured testimony, and prison sentences were imposed.

The most famous case involving a government employee grew out of information provided by Whittaker Chambers, a journalist and confessed Soviet agent. Chambers told the Senate Subcommittee that for years his source of classified information had been Alger Hiss, a State Department official who had been one of Roosevelt's advisers at the Yalta Conference and Secretary-General of the San Francisco Conference that drafted the United Nations charter. Hiss denied the charge and swore he had never seen Chambers during the period he was accused of having divulged secrets that Chambers passed on to the Russians. A 1948 federal grand jury believed Hiss's sworn testimony to be false and indicted him for perjury. He was convicted and sentenced to five years imprisonment.

Soviet intelligence successfully reached into the Justice Department to recruit an agent. Judith Coplon, employed in the department's Foreign Agents Registration Section, was arrested in New York on March 4, 1949, in the company of Valentine A. Gubitchev, a Soviet citizen employed at the United Nations. The FBI charged that at the time of her arrest Miss Coplon was carrying summaries of confidential reports to which she had access. She was convicted of espionage and sentenced to ten years in prison. In addition, she and Gubitchev were convicted for conspiracy to commit espionage and sentenced to 15 years each. Gubitchev's sentence was suspended on condition that he leave the United States and never return. Miss Coplon won a reversal on technical grounds and a new trial was ordered. However, the government felt that its case had been weakened by court rulings with relation to certain evidence and did not again take the case to court.

The headline case, of all the spy cases turned up by the FBI, was that of Rudolph Ivanovich Abel. Abel was a colonel in the Soviet State Security Service. The first break in his case occurred when a Brooklyn newspaper boy, collecting from his customers, was given a hollow nickel that contained a coded message. The FBI spent almost four years trying to decode the message and find its source. The second break came when Reino Hayhanem, a lieutenant colonel of the Soviet secret service, asked for asylum because he had been ordered back to Moscow and feared reprisals for failures in his espionage assignments. The FBI followed trails that led to a studio in Brooklyn, near where the newsboy had gotten the nickel, which was "a virtual museum of modern espionage equipment, such as short wave radios, cipher pads, cameras and film for producing microdots, a hollow shaving brush, cuff links and other 'trick' containers." Abel was arrested as he entered the studio, convicted in October, 1957, and sentenced to 30 years. In 1962, he was exchanged for the American U-2 pilot, Francis Gary Powers, who was charged by the Russians with spying on them from the sky.

Slavery and the Law

Attorneys general were very much involved in questions arising out of slavery.

The Continental Congress had prohibited slavery in the Northwest Territory and in 1794 Congress banned the building or equipping in the United States of vessels for the slave trade. The first big slave trade case arose in 1838 when Felix Grundy of Tennessee was the attorney general. A Spanish schooner, the Amistad, had sailed from Havana to another port in Cuba, then Spanish territory, with a cargo of slaves. The slaves revolted, killed the captain and forced two Spaniards, Ruiz and Montez, to promise they would sail back to Africa. But instead they sailed for the American coast, where the ship was seized by the U.S. brig, Washington. Ruiz and Montez filed a libel against the Washington, claiming the slaves as their property. The Spanish government demanded the return of the Amistad and the slaves as the property of Spanish subjects. Attorney General Grundy advised that the ship and the Negroes should be turned over to the Spanish authorities to adjudicate the claims of Ruiz and Montez. A federal district court at New Haven, Connecticut, however, rejected the claim of Ruiz and Montez, on the grounds that the Negroes had been imported from Africa in violation of Spanish law, and directed that they be returned to Africa. The United States government, on behalf of Spain, appealed to the circuit court. Grundy resigned while the appeal was pending and Henry D. Gilpin, a Philadelphia lawyer, became attorney general. The circuit court affirmed the district court so Gilpin took the case to the Supreme Court and argued it there. John Quincy Adams, former President, was retained to represent the Negroes. The Supreme Court ruled that Negroes were free and could not be forced to return.

Beginning in the 1850s, fugitive slaves became a real problem for attorneys general. The Fugitive Slave Acts of 1793, which required that slaves be returned to their owners, had been practically nullified because Northern states refused to enforce them. In 1850 a stiffer law was passed and President Fillmore signed it on the advice of Attorney General Crittenden. Seven years later a case brought under the stronger law was to reach out into much broader areas and add fuel to the fire that flamed into the Civil War.

The Dred Scott Case

This was the famous Dred Scott case of 1857 involving the return of a fugitive slave to the then Territory of Missouri. The Supreme Court's decision went beyond the question of the mere return of a slave to his master. Speaking for the Court, Chief Justice Taney, a former attorney general, laid down the doctrine that Negroes were not citizens as defined in the Constitution and therefore did not have its protection, and that Congress had no power to regulate slavery in the territories. The Taney decision relied in part upon an opinion given in 1854 by Attorney General Cushing to the effect that fugitive slaves could be reclaimed under the laws of the states, territories, and organized possessions of the United States.

The Secession Question

After Dred Scott, secession began to loom more ominously. In 1860, President James Buchanan asked Attorney General Jeremiah S. Black for an opinion on his powers to deal with the secession problem. In a significant ruling, Black held that in their respective spheres the federal and state governments were supreme and each was powerless to go beyond the limits set by the Constitution. He held that if a state should declare its independence, the President could not recognize that independence or absolve the state from its federal obligations. On the other hand, Black declared, the federal government could not make war on a state, and any attempt to do so would amount to expulsion from the union and absolve the state from federal obligations. The government could lawfully repel direct aggression on its property and officers, he said, but could not undertake an offensive war to punish the people of a state for the political misdeeds of their state government. The ruling virtually left the federal government powerless to prevent secession. Its foes called Black a traitor and the author of "Buchanan's secessionist doctrine." Black later became Secretary of State and supported a firm policy toward the South. However, when President Buchanan nominated him to the Supreme Court the Senate refused confirmation.

Lincoln's Legal Problems

As federal authority faded in the South with the refusal of judges and juries to enforce federal laws and the refusal of many lawyers to accept judicial appointments, problems pressed more heavily upon President Lincoln and his attorney general, Edward Bates of Missouri. Bates had been a candidate for President in the convention that nominated Lincoln. A native Virginian who wished to avoid war with the South, he advised Lincoln not to send provisions to Fort Sumter because it might make war inevitable. He thought the South could be subjugated without bloodshed by closing Southern ports—a close cousin of the theory that was expounded a century later during the Cuban missile crisis. Bates' patience grew thin, however, when Marylanders rioted to prevent Union troops from passing through Baltimore. Many Marylanders were arrested and held without charges and Bates advised Lincoln that his power to suspend habeas corpus arose out of his obligation to suppress insurrection. Congress later upheld Lincoln's suspension of habeas corpus as a wartime measure and when Chief Justice Taney issued writs for the release of the Marylanders, Lincoln refused to honor them. Bates consistently opposed the extension of military jurisdiction into fields of civil authority and, when he resigned and returned to Missouri, he wrote pamphlets and made angry speeches condemning usurpation of civil authority by the military. It is also interesting to note that in a departure from the Dred Scott doctrine, Bates advised Secretary of State Chase that freemen of color, if born in the United States, were citizens.

James Speed of Kentucky succeeded Bates and, when Lincoln was assassinated, Speed ruled that the conspirators could be tried in military courts. For this opinion, Bates called him an "imbecile." A little later, Speed took a different position with regard to the trial for treason of Jefferson Davis, President of the Confederacy, holding that treason trials must be in civil courts. Speed's opinion on the trial of Lincoln's assassins was the shortest—28 words—ever written by an attorney general. It read:

> SIR:—I am of the opinion that the persons charged with the murder of the President of the United States can be rightfully tried by a military court.

As far as the attorney general's office was concerned, the problems of the reconstruction era largely involved confiscation cases. A law known as the Captured and Abandoned Property Act permitted claimants to sue and recover property if they could demonstrate loyalty to the Union. The attorney general was engaged for almost 30 years in defending confiscation claims in the courts. In many of them he relied upon the archives of the Confederacy to show that claimants protesting loyalty had, in fact, been secessionists during the war.

Civil Rights

Civil rights questions became a serious concern for the attorneys general after the war, as Negroes were given citizenship and the protection of the Constitution and as the federal government attempted to enforce their new rights. Congress passed a Civil Rights Act providing that liberated slaves would be citizens, have equal rights in holding property and equal privileges in the courts. President Andrew Johnson vetoed the bill but Congress passed it over the veto.

Henry Stanbery of Ohio had succeeded Speed as attorney general. He was a staunch supporter of President Johnson and when impeachment proceedings against the President were instituted, Stanbery resigned to aid in his defense. After the impeachment trial, which failed, Johnson showed his appreciation by renominating Stanbery for the attorney generalship but the Senate refused to confirm him.

After the adoption of the Fourteenth Amendment in 1868, the right to vote and to serve on juries became a pressing issue. In 1870 Congress passed the Enforcement Act designed to give effect to the Fourteenth and Fifteenth Amendments as they applied to Negroes. The statute provided for the supervision of elections for federal officers and punishment for acts that disfranchised Negroes.

The office of attorney general had become the Department of Justice and Akerman was the attorney general. Meantime Congress had passed another enforcement statute known as the Ku Klux Act. It created civil and criminal liability for violence against individuals, authorized use of the Army and Navy to suppress disturbances, and suspension of habeas corpus. Akerman obtained an appropriation of $50,000 to employ investigators to ferret out violators of the enforcement laws. Arrests were made and indictments obtained. Cases were carried to the Supreme Court and both enforcement statutes were sustained.

These laws were deeply resented in the South and convictions were hard to obtain, particularly in election fraud cases. Unrest and disorders were relatively widespread. In one instance in South Carolina, habeas corpus was suspended in October, 1871, and federal troops were sent to quell disorders. (Federal troops were also used in Louisiana.) Attorney General Williams went to South Carolina to gain first hand knowledge that would help him in directing legal proceedings. Hundreds of indictments were returned but there were few convictions. Williams came to be regarded as an extremist and when President Grant nominated him in 1873 to be chief justice of the Supreme Court, the Senate refused confirmation.

In 1896, a case involving racial segregation in railway cars came to the Supreme Court. In its first statement of the "separate but equal" doctrine, the Court held that segregation was permissible if equal facilities were provided.

Cases Since 1954

The "separate but equal" doctrine applied in civil rights cases for almost 60 years. Then on May 17, 1954, a unanimous court held—in four cases involving the right of states to maintain racially segregated schools—that "in the field of public education the doctrine of 'separate but equal' has no place." School segregation, said the opinion written by Chief Justice Earl Warren, deprived Negroes of the "equal protection of the laws guaranteed by the Fourteenth Amendment." The attorney general participated as amicus curiae in the 1954 cases and in most major civil rights cases that followed.

Although this historic decision specifically involved cases only from South Carolina, Virginia, Kansas, Delaware, and the District of Columbia, the basic precedent is applicable in other cases involving public educational facilities throughout the nation. As Negroes attempted to enter previously all-white schools, there was strong resistance, often supported by the highest state authorities. Serious trouble developed in many towns and cities, particularly in the South, when parents, school officials, and others resisted court orders to integrate.

President Dwight Eisenhower's attorney general, Herbert Brownell, Jr., took the position that when court orders were defied, it was the duty of the Justice Department to enforce compliance by all necessary legal and constitutional means. In doing so, he used powers and procedures not invoked since reconstruction days.

The first explosive situation developed at Little Rock, Arkansas. There, the governor of the state, Orval E. Faubus, used his official position to prevent integration of a high school. President Eisenhower asked Brownell for an opinion on the President's powers for dealing with this situation. Brownell advised that the attorney general could petition for an injunction against a governor who obstructed a court's orders. He also advised that the President could call the National Guard of a state into federal service and use it with other armed forces to suppress domestic violence and resistance to judicial mandates. Acting upon his advice, President Eisenhower federalized the Arkansas National Guard, thus removing it from the control of Governor Faubus who had mobilized it to enforce his policies, and also dispatched federal troops to Little Rock. Eventually an uneasy calm was restored and a few Negro students were admitted to the Little Rock high school.

The following year, when the schools reopened in Little Rock, again there was resistance and public disorder. This time, instead of sending troops, the Department of Justice, then headed by Attorney General William P. Rogers, used United States marshals to reinforce local law enforcement officers, a procedure less repugnant to the South. In both Little Rock situations, FBI agents were active in investigative phases.

Federal troops, United States marshals, a strong FBI contingent, and Justice Department attorneys working under direction of Attorney General Kennedy were used again in 1962 when Governor Ross Barnett spearheaded resistance to court orders to admit James Meredith, a Negro, to the University of Mississippi. There were riots, murder, and bloodshed on the university campus and, even after Meredith was admitted, marshals guarded him for many weeks. The University of Mississippi situation emphasized federal determination to uphold civil rights as defined by laws and courts against the concept of states' rights.

Civil rights cases flowing from the Supreme Court's school decision piled up in the courts and Negroes pressed for full integration. The Civil Rights Division of the Department of Justice, newly created by the Civil Rights Act of 1957, had its hands full. In the Rogers administration a vigorous effort was made to protect voting rights of Negroes. The particular objective was to prevent local officials from using discriminatory practices against Negroes seeking to register and vote. Many prosecutions were instituted, injunctions obtained, and cases argued through district and circuit courts to the Supreme Court, where rulings were uniformly in the government's favor.

Step by step, the Supreme Court outlawed segregation in interstate transportation, public parks, swimming pools, beaches and places of amusement. White resistance to this gradual breaking down of a traditional way of life led to renewed disorders and ugly crimes. Participants in "freedom marches" and other demonstrations, both white and colored, clashed with police and were jailed. Convictions under local laws and ordinances were challenged as denying rights guaranteed by the Constitution and moved in increasing volume to the Supreme Court where they usually were reversed.

The Civil Rights Act of 1957 was the first passed by Congress in almost a century. It gave the Department of Justice authority to act in areas hitherto not clearly defined and, under it, Attorney General Rogers and his successor Robert Kennedy stepped up efforts for which Negroes were clamoring ever more loudly. The Civil Rights Act of 1960 further expanded the Justice Department's jurisdiction. But these laws did not satisfy the civil rights movement, which was demanding faster progress toward complete racial equality. In 1963 President John F. Kennedy sent to Congress new proposals designed to give the Justice Department additional weapons for combatting discrimination. After a prolonged filibuster and determined pressure from the new President, Lyndon Johnson, these proposals emerged as the Civil Rights Act of 1964. Its principal new features were the provision of a Fair Employment Practices Commission and a ban on discrimination in public accommodations, such as stores, restaurants, hotels, and other service facilities. The constitutionality of these provisions was challenged and as the law went into effect, it became clear that it would engage the courts and law enforcement agencies in litigation for many years.

Credit Mobilier and the Iron Horse

When restless settlers eager for land started moving into territories ceded by Mexico or acquired through the Louisiana Purchase, the law followed them—although it was not always able to keep them in sight. For decades the Justice Department was involved in suits to quiet or establish title, in claims to mineral, timber, and water rights, in boundary suits and the rights and claims of Indian tribes. Fifty cases involving the Louisiana Purchase territories alone went to the Supreme Court, and there were many others from California and other Western and Southern states. Twenty-six went to the Supreme Court in the second administration of Attorney General Crittenden. (He won all of them.) By 1870, most of the land cases had been settled and the department's activities in that phase of the development of the west slackened.

But in the early 1870s the Credit Mobilier affair, which became a scandal in President Grant's 1872 campaign, gave the Justice Department some difficult legal and political problems.

During the Civil War, Congress had chartered the Union Pacific Railroad Company and granted it money and public lands to enable it to push westward to meet the Central Pacific pushing eastward from California. In accordance with usual practice, Union Pacific let the contract to build the line to a private company, Credit Mobilier. It was dominated by Oliver Ames & Sons, powerful New England financiers and its president, Oakes Ames, was a member of Congress. His brother, Oliver, became president of Union Pacific. Whispers of fraud and corruption in connection with Credit Mobilier's operations began to be heard and a congressional investigation threatened. Perhaps to avoid it, Congressman Ames allowed some fellow legislators to acquire Credit Mobilier shares for a small part of their value. Nevertheless, Congress directed the attorney general to determine if the Union Pacific and Central Pacific might have forfeited their charters and franchises, or paid illegal dividends and if their directors, agents, and employees had violated any law. Powerful financial interests were at work in political circles, however, and no specific action was taken.

The matter became an issue in the 1872 campaign, and the major question by then involved the interest due on the large government loans to the railroads—that is, whether the railroads had to pay the interest currently or at the end of 30 years when the loans matured. The secretary of the treasury argued that since the interest was compounded semi-annually, it was due semi-annually, and that the Treasury Department had authority to withhold unpaid interest from moneys due the railroads for transportation services. Attorney General Akerman sustained him. The railroads contended that no interest was due until the 30-year life of the loans expired. More than $5,000,000 in claimed interest was at stake.

Early in 1873, the House of Representatives asked President Grant to bring suit to collect the unpaid interest. Later that year, an Appropriations Act directed the Treasury to withhold money due the railroads for services and to sue the railroads and other persons who had received bonds, money, or lands through fraudulent contracts or otherwise. Earlier, Senator George H. Williams of Oregon had opposed investigation of Credit Mobilier but now, as attorney general, he obtained an injunction against the Union Pacific and Credit Mobilier to prevent further waste of resources while the suit was pending.

The case reached a federal circuit court in October, 1873. Attorney General Williams participated in the argument. William Maxwell Evarts of New York, who later became attorney general, was a lawyer for the defense. The circuit court found for the railroads, holding that the loans were not yet due. The government appealed to the Supreme Court and the case was twice argued in that tribunal. In 1878, five years after the circuit court's decision, the high court upheld the lower court's ruling. Meantime a court of claims' decision that the interest was not due until the end of the 30-year period had been sustained by the Supreme Court. Eventually the railroads agreed to issue bonds that the government could sell to discharge the debt.

Williams supervised the case through the courts but it was his predecessor, Akerman, who took the political rap. The railroads had sought to extend their lines into new territory and receive grants of land. Akerman advised President Grant that this could not be done without specific legislation, an opinion that aroused such hostility from the railroads that Grant requested his resignation.

Protection of Natural Resources

The problems of the west have continued to engage the legislative and executive branches of the government, particularly the law enforcement agencies, right up to the present time. In the more recent years, however, the major issues have centered on conservation of resources. These led to troubles with cattlemen and sheepmen, lumbermen, oil interests, railroads, homesteaders, and Indians.

Conservation became a burning issue in the administration of Theodore Roosevelt. Gifford Pinchot, a crusader to save the forests, was head of the Department of Agriculture's Division of Forestry. Along with others, he asserted that the policy of disposing of government lands to private owners had resulted in forests being stripped, mines looted, grazing lands exhausted, homesteads illegally obtained and the exploiters of these resources outrageously enriched—all at the expense of the general public. Supported by the President, Pinchot stirred public interest in establishing reserves to conserve forests and other resources. When the reserves were created, attorneys general were called upon to prosecute such offenses as illegal grazing, setting fires in forests, stealing water and timber, and unlawful homesteading (including the practice of entering land for homestead purposes with the intent of selling to lumber companies or other large scale operators).

Teapot Dome

Oil reserves were not involved at first but the Teapot Dome scandal and the submerged lands controversy brought them into the picture. Albert B. Fall, secretary of the interior in the cabinet of President Warren G. Harding, granted the Doheny interests leases to take oil from Teapot Dome, a naval reserve. Harding's attorney general, Harry M. Daugherty, had no part in granting the leases but when a congressional investigation disclosed corruption in connection with the deals, he came under attack and demands were made for his impeachment. A House Judiciary Committee exonerated him but the attacks in Congress continued and the Senate appointed a special committee to inquire into his official conduct. Calvin Coolidge, who succeeded to the presidency upon the death of Harding, was embarrassed by the scandals of the Harding Administration. He requested and received Daugherty's resignation. Subsequently, bribery charges were lodged against Fall and Edward L. Doheny, head of the Doheny interests. Fall was convicted and served a prison term; Doheny was acquitted.

Tidelands Cases

An issue of federal versus states' rights was involved in the submerged lands, or tidelands, cases. Lands beneath the coastal waters of California and the Gulf of Mexico were rich in deposits of oil and other minerals. The federal government leased tidelands oil resources to private operators and collected the royalties. The Submerged Lands Act of 1953, which fixed the boundaries of state ownership at the three-mile limit, had been upheld by the Supreme Court. But Louisiana elected to test the law on the claim that its boundaries extended three marine leagues, or about ten and a half miles, seaward from the shore and that it was entitled to ownership and control of oil and other minerals of those lands, and to the revenues therefrom. The government contended that state boundaries could not extend beyond the traditional three-mile limit. J. Lee Rankin, the solicitor general, won a victory when the Supreme Court decided that the Submerged Lands Act did not confer upon the states control of underwater areas beyond the three-mile limit.

The Bank of the United States

From Alexander Hamilton to Andrew Jackson the question of a central bank was a political and legal issue. The first official opinion on the question was given to George Washington by Randolph who advised that Congress did not have power to establish a national bank. Congress chartered one, nevertheless, and for decades titans of the times fought legal and legislative battles over it. The landmark case was *McCulloch* v. *Maryland.*

The first charter of the Bank of the United States expired in 1811. The case of *McCulloch* v. *Maryland* came to the Supreme Court in 1819 as a test of a bill signed by President Madison on April 10, 1816, permitting rechartering. The issue was whether Congress had authority under the Constitution to incorporate a bank and whether the bank had authority to establish a branch in Baltimore without Maryland's consent. Maryland claimed the right to tax the branch bank's revenues. Attorney General William Wirt was associated with Daniel Webster and William Pinkney, a former attorney general, in conducting the government's case. Wirt and Webster argued that legislative, executive, and judicial acts since 1811 had treated the banks as lawfully established. Wirt said that the power to create a bank "must be considered as ratified by the voice of the people and sanctioned by precedent." When Webster asserted that Maryland could not tax the bank's notes, Joseph Hopkinson, arguing for Maryland, pointed out that the federal government taxed state banks.

The government won in an opinion by Chief Justice Marshall. He ruled that the "sound construction of the Constitution must allow to the national legislature that discretion . . . which will enable that body to perform the high duties assigned to it in the manner most beneficial to the people." Any legitimate means that were not prohibited but "consistent with the letter and spirit of the Constitution," Marshall said, were constitutional. On the taxing power, Marshall upheld the supremacy of federal law, stating that "the whole might tax the part but the part might not tax the whole."

The controversy continued, however, and one of the most implacable opponents of the Bank of the United States was Andrew Jackson. In his first message to Congress as President, in 1829, Jackson said that the bank had failed "in the great end of establishing a uniform and sound currency." He suggested, instead, a national institution founded on government credit and revenues. Attorney General John McPherson Berrien, of Georgia, opposed Jackson's views—whereupon he was fired and replaced with Taney, who distrusted the bank's power over finances as much as Jackson did. Nicholas Biddle, president of the bank, was pressing Congress for a new charter, even though the current one had a few years to run. This time the recharter proposal had the support of Henry Clay, as well as Webster—both of whom were less interested in the bank than in weakening Jackson politically. Taney was the principal drafter of Jackson's message vetoing the recharter bill. The message repudiated the *McCulloch* v. *Maryland* doctrine that constitutionality had been settled by precedent and declared that the Supreme Court must not be permitted to control Congress or the executive branch when acting in their proper capacities.

The re-election of Jackson sealed the bank's fate. The President sought to terminate the government's relationship with the bank by withdrawing federal deposits and asked Taney if he had power to do so. Taney ruled that he could withdraw the deposits and require the secretary of the treasury to designate state banks as depositaries. Jackson appointed Taney secretary of the treasury, and he withdrew the deposits and set up a system of state depositaries. Taney's appointment was ad interim, however, and when Jackson submitted it formally for confirmation, the Senate refused. This was the first time a cabinet appointment had been rejected by the Senate. Jackson then tried to reward Taney by naming him an associate justice of the Supreme Court but again a hostile Senate rejected him. With the next election, the composition of the Senate changed. Thereupon, Jackson nominated Taney to succeed Marshall as chief justice of the United States; he was confirmed in 1836 and held the position until his death in 1864.

"Trust-Busting"

Ever since Credit Mobilier, through the "trust-busting" days of Teddy Roosevelt and down to the present, attorneys general have been involved in actions and policies relating to the conduct or misconduct of business organizations and businessmen. Monopoly in restraint of trade, mergers tending to create monopoly, price-fixing, rate-making and other practices made illegal by statute have been their concern. Enforcement of the Sherman Act, the Clayton Act, the Robinson-Patman Act, and other statutes has touched almost every segment of industry and commerce.

One of the earliest problems grew out of Alexander Graham Bell's invention of the telegraph in 1844 and the telephone in 1876. The American Bell Telephone Company and the Western Union Telegraph Company were soon in litigation over patents but settled the dispute out of court, with Western Union conceding that the Bell patents were valid and withdrawing from the telephone field. The telephone business expanded rapidly. Rumbles about exorbitant rates were heard from the public and there was talk of state regulation of rates. Independent companies claiming to hold patents that antedated Bell's sprang up and it appeared that the Justice Department would sue to annul Bell patents. It was disclosed, however, that Attorney General Garland was a stockholder in Pan-Electric Telephone Company, one of the independents. When Garland was urged to sue to vacate the Bell patents he went on vacation, leaving Solicitor General John Goode to authorize the suit. President Grover Cleveland called

Garland back to Washington to explain his interest in a competing company and subsequently the suit, which had been filed in Tennessee, was withdrawn.

Later suits were filed in Ohio, where Bell challenged the court's jurisdiction and won, and in Massachusetts where Bell again won on the point that the government lacked authority to annul a patent without specific legislation. When the Massachusetts case reached the Supreme Court, the jurisdiction of the government and the right to sue to cancel a patent obtained by fraud, accident, or mistake were upheld. The case went back to the lower court for trial on the issue of whether injury to the public had resulted from illegal granting of patent rights. Meantime, in 1892 while testimony in the case was being taken, Bell's basic patents expired. There were further legal delays and in 1895 Attorney General Judson Harmon laid the problem before Congress. The Congress was reluctant to advise in an atmosphere antagonistic to big corporations and the case remained on the docket for ten more years, until 1906, when it was dismissed.

Bell Telephone continued to expand but, by 1908, there were also 12,000 independent telephone companies. Bell began cutting off connections with the independents.

The American Telephone and Telegraph Company had been organized as the operating company of the Bell system. AT&T also dominated Western Union, the same man heading both companies. There were insistent demands for government action against the alleged monopoly and Attorney General Wickersham asked AT&T to suspend certain actions, such as acquisition of independent companies, until the Justice Department had completed an investigation. No suit was brought but, in late 1913, AT&T agreed to dispose of its stock in Western Union, to cease its efforts to acquire competing telephone lines and to connect its long distance lines with the local exchanges of the independent companies. In 1921, Congress passed legislation permitting merger of telephone properties with the approval of the Interstate Commerce Commission.

Philander C. Knox was attorney general in 1902 when an indictment was returned against Northern Securities Company, involving a proposed merger of the Great Northern, Northern Pacific, and the Chicago, Burlington and Quincy railroads. Financial giants like E. H. Harriman and James J. Hill were key figures in the merger.

Knox supervised the case up through the Supreme Court and argued it there. He won a judgment against the company. Later Knox drafted legislation creating the Department of Commerce and Labor and was one of the drafters of the law giving the ICC effective control of railroad rates.

The Teddy Roosevelt "trust-busting" drive reached its peak under Attorney General William H. Moody, Knox's successor. Moody personally directed the so-called *Beef Trust* case against the big Chicago meat packers and he instituted prosecutions alleging restraint of trade against combinations in the paper, fertilizer, salt, tobacco, oil, lumber, and other industries. Charles J. Bonaparte, who followed Moody, instituted 20 antitrust suits and won eight of them. In the Taft Administration, Attorney General George Wickersham made the closing arguments in the Supreme Court in the government's suit to dissolve the Union Pacific-Southern Pacific merger and in the Standard Oil and American Tobacco Company cases. In these two latter cases the Supreme Court laid down its historic "rule of reason" doctrine, which has applied to many later antitrust cases. During the incumbency of James C. McReynolds, who served briefly as Woodrow Wilson's first attorney general, a decree dissolving the Union Pacific-Southern Pacific merger was handed down; and decrees were also obtained requiring the New Haven Railroad to relinquish its transportation monopoly in New England, dissolving the United States Thread Association, requiring AT&T to relinquish its monopoly of wire communications, restraining the National Wholesale Jewelers Association from conspiracy in restraint of trade, and prohibiting the Elgin (Illinois) Board of Trade from continuing certain price-fixing practices.

There were peaks and valleys in antitrust enforcement in the years preceding and during World War II. Generally, the government took a lenient view toward companies that produced war materiel and, in certain instances, it sanctioned collective operations. Some cases were filed and litigated, however, one being against the United States Steel Company. The government lost this case, the Supreme Court holding that mere size of a corporation was not proof of illegal monopoly, that actual restraint of trade, and not just the capacity to restrain, must be proved. With wartime considerations out of the way, President Eisenhower's attorneys general, first Brownell and then Rogers, filed hundreds of suits involving the automobile, rubber, drug, radio, motion picture, aluminum, electrical, and other industries, and some international cartels. The most widely publicized case was against General Electric, Westinghouse, and other big electrical manufacturers for conspiracy to fix prices. The companies avoided trial by nolo contendere pleas but were fined heavily, and several of their officers were fined and sent to jail.

The government's power to regulate business and commerce was strengthened in 1899 by an opinion that Attorney General John W. Griggs wrote for President William McKinley. Griggs held that, under the commerce clause of the Constitution, the power of the United States to regulate commerce in general was absolute and without limit—either as to time, place, or details of exercise—except as to navigable waters lying wholly within the boundaries of a state. He said that the power included the right to regulate all means and instrumentalities used in commerce and was not restricted to purchase, sale or barter of commodities but included navigation, transportation, etc.

Presidential Inability

The assassination of President James A. Garfield gave rise to the first serious consideration of the problem of who performs the duties of the President when he is incapacitated. The Constitution provided that the Vice President shall succeed to the powers and duties of the presidency in the event of death or incapacity of the President. It did not, however, settle the question of how to determine when a President is unable to perform his duties. Garfield lingered for months after being shot by Charles Guiteau but Vice President Chester A. Arthur declined to assume the presidential office as long as Garfield was alive. Similarly, when Woodrow Wilson's health failed and he was not fully able to perform his duties, Vice President Thomas Marshall did not assert his constitutional prerogative. More than 30 years later, when President Eisenhower suffered three serious illnesses clamor arose for a constitutional settlement of the question. Attorney General Rogers took the position that a constitutional amendment was not necessary and helped work out a written understanding between the President and Vice President Richard M. Nixon. Its principal elements were that the President would decide when he could not do his job and the Vice President would then take over, but that when the President decided he was able to resume the office, the Vice President would relinquish it. In 1961, Attorney General Kennedy ruled that the memo embodying the arrangement between Eisenhower and Nixon was a correct interpretation of Article II, Section I, Clause 6 of the Constitution. That clause authorized the Vice President to act as President and discharge the powers and duties of the office "until the disability be removed." The death of President Kennedy stirred renewed agitation for legislative action and in 1965 Congress approved a constitutional amendment to resolve the question. This was ratified, and it was certified as the 25th Amendment on February 25, 1967.

Epilogue

It will be obvious from what has been written above that men who have held the office of attorney general have woven binding threads into the fabric of history and have participated as statesmen or as counselors of statesmen in events that have shaped the policies and destinies of the nation. All have been the government's lawyers, but their zeal has been tempered by the creed inscribed above the office of the attorney general that "The United States wins its case whenever justice is done one of its citizens in the courts."

The law, however, has not always been their primary interest. Some have been more interested and better qualified for diplomacy, politics or even other administrative positions in the executive department. Some have held such positions before or after serving as attorney general. Some have gone on to the Supreme Court.

Those who became justices of the Supreme Court—ten in all— were Roger Brooke Taney, Nathan Clifford, Edwin M. Stanton, Joseph McKenna, William H. Moody, James C. McReynolds, Harlan F. Stone, Frank Murphy, Robert H. Jackson, and Tom C. Clark. Taney and Stone served as chief justice.

Attorneys general who served in cabinet offices other than as head of the Justice Department were Edmund Randolph, Jeremiah S. Black, Richard Olney and Philander C. Knox as secretaries of state; Richard Rush and Taney as secretaries of the treasury; John Y. Mason, Isaac Toucey, Moody, and Charles Bonaparte as secretaries of the navy, and Stanton and Alphonso Taft as secretaries of war.

Diplomatic posts were held by Caesar Augustus Rodney, minister to Argentina; William Pinkney, minister to Russia; Rush, minister to Great Britain and minister to France; Hugh S. Legare, charge d'affaires, Belgium; Mason, minister to France; Reverdy Johnson, minister to Great Britain; Caleb Cushing, minister to Spain; Edwards Pierrepont, minister to Great Britain; John Nelson, minister to the Two Sicilies (the Court of Naples); Alphonso Taft, minister to Austria and minister to Russia; and Wayne MacVeagh, minister to Turkey and ambassador to Italy. It will be noted that the practice of appointing attorneys general to diplomatic posts died out after MacVeagh, who became ambassador to Italy in 1893, 12 years after his term as attorney general. It would have been revived in 1964 if President Lyndon Johnson had accepted Robert Kennedy's offer to serve as ambassador to South Vietnam.

Thirteen attorneys general were United States senators, either before or after service as head of the law enforcement office. They were Breckenridge, Rodney, Pinkney, Berrien, Grundy, Crittenden, Toucey, Johnson, Evarts, Williams, Garland, Knox, and Robert F. Kennedy.

Levi Lincoln, Rodney, Pinkney, Grundy, Crittenden, Legare, Nelson, Mason, Clifford, Toucey, Cushing, Bates, McKenna, Moody, and Palmer served in the House of Representatives.

Attorneys general who were governors of states were Randolph (Virginia), Lincoln (Massachusetts), Crittenden (Kentucky), Toucey (Connecticut), Garland (Arkansas), Judson Harmon (Ohio), John William Greggs (New Jersey), and Murphy (Michigan).

ATTORNEYS GENERAL OF
THE UNITED STATES—1789-1968

	State	President
Edmund Randolph September 26, 1789-January 2, 1794	Virginia	Washington
William Bradford January 27, 1794-August 23, 1795	Pennsylvania	Washington
Charles Lee December 10, 1795-February 18, 1801	Virginia	Washington and John Adams

	State	President
Levi Lincoln March 5, 1801-March 3, 1805	Massachusetts	Jefferson
John Breckenridge August 7, 1805-December 14, 1806	Kentucky	Jefferson
Caesar A. Rodney January 20, 1807-December 11, 1811	Delaware	Jefferson and Madison
William Pinkney December 11, 1811-February 10, 1814	Maryland	Madison
Richard Rush February 10, 1814-November 13, 1817	Pennsylvania	Madison
William Wirt November 13, 1817-March 3, 1829	Virginia	Monroe and John Quincy Adams
John M. Berrien March 9, 1829-July 20, 1831	Georgia	Jackson
Roger B. Taney July 20, 1831-September 4, 1833	Maryland	Jackson
Benjamin F. Butler November 15, 1833-September 1, 1838	New York	Jackson and Van Buren
Felix Grundy July 5, 1838-December 1, 1839	Tennessee	Van Buren
Henry D. Gilpin January 11, 1840-March 4, 1841	Pennsylvania	Van Buren
John J. Crittenden March 5, 1841-September 13, 1841	Kentucky	Harrison and Tyler
Hugh S. Legare September 13, 1841-June 20, 1843	South Carolina	Tyler
John Nelson July 1, 1843-March 3, 1845	Virginia	Tyler
John Y. Mason March 6, 1845-September 9, 1846	Virginia	Polk
Nathan Clifford October 17, 1846-March 17, 1848	Maine	Polk
Isaac Toucey June 21, 1848-March 3, 1849	Connecticut	Polk

	State	*President*
Reverdy Johnson March 8, 1849-July 20, 1850	Maryland	Taylor
John J. Crittenden July 22, 1850-March 3, 1853 (second term)	Kentucky	Fillmore
Caleb Cushing March 7, 1853-March 3, 1857	Massachusetts	Pierce
Jeremiah S. Black March 6, 1857-December 17, 1860	Pennsylvania	Buchanan
Edwin M. Stanton December 20, 1860-March 3, 1861	Ohio	Buchanan
Edward Bates March 5, 1861-November 24, 1864	Missouri	Lincoln
James Speed December 2, 1864-July 17, 1866	Kentucky	Lincoln and Johnson
Henry Stanbery July 23, 1866-March 12, 1868	Ohio	Johnson
William M. Evarts July 15, 1868-March 3, 1869	New York	Johnson
Ebenezer R. Hoar March 5, 1869-June 23, 1870	Massachusetts	Grant
Amos T. Akerman June 23, 1870-January 10, 1872	Georgia	Grant
George H. Williams December 14, 1871-May 15, 1875	Oregon	Grant
Edwards Pierrepont April 26, 1875-May 22, 1876	New York	Grant
Alphonso Taft May 22, 1876-March 11, 1877	Ohio	Grant
Charles Devens March 12, 1877-March 6, 1881	Massachusetts	Hayes
Wayne MacVeagh March 5, 1881-October 24, 1881	Pennsylvania	Garfield
Benjamin H. Brewster December 19, 1881-March 5, 1885	Pennsylvania	Arthur

	State	President
Augustus H. Garland March 6, 1885-March 5, 1889	Arkansas	Cleveland
William H. H. Miller March 5, 1889-March 6, 1893	Indiana	Harrison
Richard Olney March 6, 1893-June 7, 1895	Massachusetts	Cleveland
Judson Harmon June 8, 1895-March 5, 1897	Ohio	Cleveland
Joseph McKenna March 5, 1897-January 25, 1898	California	McKinley
John W. Griggs June 25, 1898-March 29, 1901	New Jersey	McKinley
Philander C. Knox April 5, 1901-June 30, 1904	Pennsylvania	McKinley
William H. Moody July 1, 1904-December 17, 1906	Massachusetts	Roosevelt
Charles J. Bonaparte December 17, 1906-March 4, 1909	Maryland	Roosevelt
George W. Wickersham March 5, 1909-March 5, 1913	New York	Taft
James C. McReynolds March 5, 1913-August 29, 1914	Tennessee	Wilson
Thomas W. Gregory August 29, 1914-March 4, 1919	Texas	Wilson
A. Mitchell Palmer March 5, 1919-March 5, 1921	Pennsylvania	Wilson
Harry M. Daugherty March 4, 1921-March 28, 1924	Ohio	Harding
Harlan Fiske Stone April 7, 1924-March 2, 1925	New York	Coolidge
John C. Sargent March 17, 1925-March 5, 1929	Vermont	Coolidge
William D. Mitchell March 5, 1929-March 3, 1933	Minnesota	Hoover

	State	*President*
Homer S. Cummings March 4, 1933-January 2, 1939	Connecticut	Roosevelt
Frank Murphy January 2, 1939-January 18, 1940	Michigan	Roosevelt
Robert H. Jackson January 18, 1940-July 10, 1941	New York	Roosevelt
Francis Biddle September 5, 1941-June 30, 1945	Pennsylvania	Roosevelt
Tom C. Clark June 15, 1945-August 24, 1949	Texas	Truman
J. Howard McGrath August 24, 1949-April 7, 1952	Rhode Island	Truman
James P. McGranery May 27, 1952-January 20, 1953	Pennsylvania	Truman
Herbert Brownell, Jr. January 21, 1953-November 8, 1957	New York	Eisenhower
William P. Rogers November 8, 1957-January 20, 1961	Maryland	Eisenhower
Robert F. Kennedy January 21, 1961-September 3, 1964	Massachusetts	Kennedy
Nicholas de B. Katzenbach September 4, 1964-October 2, 1966	Illinois	Johnson
Ramsey Clark March 3, 1967-	Texas	Johnson

ACKNOWLEDGMENTS

In the preparation of this paper the author has drawn upon the following works and acknowledges indebtedness to the authors thereof:

Federal Justice, by former Attorney General Homer S. Cummings.

"The Department of Justice, Its Origin, Development and Present Day Organization," by Frank Buckley, *Boston University Law Review,* January 1925.

"Office and Duties of the Attorney General," by Caleb Cushing, *American Law Register,* December, 1856.

"The Opinion Function of the Federal Government," by Rita W. Nealon, *New York University Law Review,* 1950.

"The United States Department of Justice," by John A. Fairlie, *Michigan Law Review,* 1905.

"The Office of The Attorney General," by Tom C Clark, *Tennessee Law Review,* 1946.

The Opinions of The Attorneys General in the library of the Department of Justice.

Biographical Sketches of the Attorneys General, by Arthur Robb, 1946.

The United States Department of Justice; A brief Account of its Organization and Activities, by Attorney General Robert F. Kennedy, January, 1961.

As a reporter covering the Justice Department for many years, and as one who served four years as Director of Public Information for the department, the author also has used extensively information from his own files and experience.

II.

THE ATTORNEY GENERAL AS THE PRESIDENT'S LAWYER

By Arthur Selwyn Miller

THE CHIEF LEGAL OFFICER of the United States government is the attorney general. As a member of the cabinet, he necessarily has close and continuing relationships with the President. As head of one of the major departments of government, he is in charge of a vast and complex system—"the largest law office in the world."

But the attorney general is more than merely a lawyer and counsellor, as the following exposition will indicate. To outline the duties of his office and his relationships with the chief executive requires that preliminary attention be paid to certain basic attributes of American society. The introduction to this chapter sketches that background. Following it is a discussion of the attorney general as a "collectivity"—as an organization, that is, rather than as an individual. After that will be found a number of examples of the manner in which the attorney general serves the President. One conclusion should be mentioned at the outset: that the relationship is one of great complexity, when it is seen in its entirety. What gets public attention is usually the tip of the iceberg, underneath which may be discerned a vast number of ways in which the chief law officer of the government functions within the governmental structure. Other conclusions will be set forth at the end of this chapter.

Introduction

That the American people are legalistic in nature has long been noted by commentators. Well over a century ago, Alexis de Tocqueville, in his definitive study *Democracy in America,* set forth the seminal exposition of the role that law and lawyers have had in the development of the United States. In the course of this exposition he made what has since become one of the most quoted statements from that book: "Scarcely any political question arises in the United States that is not resolved, sooner or later, into a judicial question." Political questions, in other words, tend in the American system to become legal questions. It is that characteristic of our polity that provides a useful point of departure for an exposition of the attorney general of the United States and his role as the "President's lawyer."

One reason for the central position of law in the United States is the Constitution itself. Written in 1787 and amended only two dozen times since, it is the oldest fundamental law in the world. The United States has the rare good fortune of having the oldest continuous governmental structure extant today. (The only competitor for that honor is Great Britain, and there the immense changes in limiting the monarchy during the past two centuries have made that nation basically different from what it was as recently as 1800.)

Having a *written* constitution, moreover, made it necessary to have some method whereby governmental acts could be tested for consonance with that constitution. Under the American system, the judiciary—and ultimately the Supreme Court of the United States—has the task of determining whether given actions by both state and the national government are valid. That does not mean, it should be emphasized, that the Court reviews *all* acts of government, but rather only those fitting the rigid requirements of "justiciability."

The Constitution divides the responsibilities of government—first, in the federal system, as between the states and the central government, and second, within the central government itself in the tripartite division of powers (legislative, executive, and judicial). This is a highly complex way of organizing a nation's political system. Small wonder, then, that the American people are legalistic. And small wonder, too, that debates over the Constitution (and other law) are often at the center of public attention. As *The Economist*

(London) said in 1952 when President Truman ordered the seizure of the steel industry (a move later declared unconstitutional by the Supreme Court):

> At the first sound of a new argument over the United States Constitution and its interpretation the hearts of Americans leap with a fearful joy. The blood stirs powerfully in their veins and a new lustre brightens their eyes. Like King Harry's men before Harfleur, they stand like greyhounds in the slips, straining upon the start.

Another factor is important as background; in addition to being legalistic by nature, the American people, committed to the democratic principle of government, have invested various government officials with the difficult task of determining what the law *should* be as well as what it *is*. As Professor Frank H. Knight, the well-known University of Chicago economist, has put it: "Democracy has assumed the task, enormously more difficult than enforcing a law known to all, of deciding what the law ought to be and making any changes called for." Within the national government, Congress is the branch which sets the general tone that public policy takes. But the Supreme Court, as recent opinions in such matters as school prayers and legislative apportionment vividly illustrate, also has had a part to play. Furthermore, the third branch of government—the executive or administrative branch—ever increasingly participates in the law-creating functions. It is here that the President and his key legal adviser, the attorney general, have in the past often set national policy in important areas of public concern. There is more to the job of being attorney general, that is to say, than taking part in lawsuits before the courts or in interpreting statutes (the legislative will).

The basic importance of the President's lawyer in the governmental structure has been characteristic of our entire constitutional history. During the very first session of Congress after the Constitution was promulgated, the Judiciary Act of 1789 was enacted. This statute provided, among other things, for the appointment of "a meet person, learned in the law, to act as attorney general for the United States." That person was to be given the following generalized duties:

> . . . to prosecute and conduct all suits in the Supreme Court in which the United States shall be concerned, and

to give his advice and opinion upon questions of law when required by the President of the United States, or when requested by heads of any of the departments, touching any matters that may concern their departments.

Soon after the Judiciary Act was passed, President Washington appointed Edmund Randolph of Virginia to be the first attorney general. For Randolph, as well as for many of his successors, the position was a part-time job which permitted him to practice law on the side. But President Washington, as succeeding chief executives have, fully recognized the key importance of the position; in a letter to Randolph, he said:

> The selection of the fittest characters to expound the laws, and dispense justice, has been the invariable object of my anxious concern. I mean not to flatter when I say that considerations like these have ruled in the nomination of the attorney general of the United States, and that my private wishes would be highly gratified by your acceptance.

The nation has come a long way since Randolph's appointment in 1789, and its development is reflected in the evolution of the attorney general's office and of the Department of Justice over which he presides.

Obviously, the Office of the Attorney General is quite different from what it was in 1789. For that matter, it is significantly different from what it was 100 years ago, for the Department of Justice was not created until 1870. And it is only in the twentieth century that the department has taken on the significance it has today.

With the above comments as background, what, then, is the role of the attorney general as the "President's lawyer"? Space limitations do not permit a full development. Nevertheless, some generalized statements can be made, augmented by reference to specific instances when the relationship between the President and the attorney general took on special significance. In addition, some reference will be made to the attorney general's relationship to other agencies and departments within the public administration—within what is loosely called the executive branch of the federal government. Finally, brief mention of the solicitor general will be set forth.

What is "the Attorney General"?

The first matter to be grasped is that the attorney general, while an individual, operates within government as a collectivity. He is to be understood as one man—and as many men. He was Edmund Randolph when George Washington was President and he is Ramsey Clark today. But today, in addition to being a member of the cabinet, he signifies thousands of lawyers, prosecutors, FBI agents, and others scattered the country over, and even overseas.

Within the headquarters of the Department of Justice in Washington, which occupies a huge building covering an entire block, are 20 principal sub-offices.

Merely listing these offices[1] suffices to indicate the great range and complexity of the responsibilities entrusted to the attorney general. In general, these responsibilities include: (1) enforcing of federal laws, (2) furnishing legal counsel in federal cases, (3) construing the laws under which the other governmental departments act, (4) conducting all suits in the Supreme Court in which the United States is concerned, (5) supervising federal penal institutions, (6) investigating and detecting violations of federal laws, (7) representing the government in legal matters generally, (8) rendering legal advice and opinions, upon request, to the President and to the heads of the executive departments, and supervising and directing the activities of (9) the United States attorneys and (10) marshals in the various judicial districts.

Speaking broadly, all of these duties involve specialized administration of acts of Congress which have been entrusted to the department. That administration is a part of the President's specific constitutional duty "to take care that the laws be faithfully executed." In legal theory, there is a direct line of authority running from the President through the attorney general to the various sub-officials of the Department of Justice. Accordingly, each of these sub-officials may be said to be assisting in executing those laws.

Obviously, only a few of these officials are directly and intimately concerned with the President and the principal point of contact is the attorney general. But the President may directly consult sub-

---

[1] See Chapter I.

ordinate officials for special reasons, for example, J. Edgar Hoover, head of the Federal Bureau of Investigation.

However, as in the case of the attorney general, the presidency is more than just one man—or even the small group of people immediately around *the President;* it, the presidency, should be viewed as an organization and not one man. When speaking of the President, one really is speaking both personally and collectively. The concept of the "institutionalized presidency" is important. It means the several hundred people who work within the Executive Office of the President, including the White House staff, the Bureau of the Budget, the Council of Economic Advisers, the National Security Council, the National Aeronautics and Space Council, the Office of Emergency Planning, the Office of Science and Technology, and the Office of the Special Representative for Trade Negotiations. In addition, the director and deputy director of the Central Intelligence Agency are part of the Executive Office of the President.

This rather large immediate official family makes up the institutionalized presidency. Just as the attorney general is a collectivity, so too is the chief executive. However, it must always be borne in mind that neither the President nor the attorney general will allow himself to be "absorbed" into these institutionalized structures to such an extent that he loses either identity or initiative. As pointed out above, the President will occasionally call on one of the attorney general's subordinates, or he may direct one of his own staff assistants to handle a matter with the attorney general.

Role of Special Counsel to the President. No study of this subject can be complete without considering the function of one presidential staff officer—or, more precisely, one presidential staff office. That is the office of special counsel to the President. Attorneys general are, as we have noted, jealous of their contacts with the President and his staff. They are especially sensitive to the possibility that the special counsel to the President, rather than the attorney general, might be regarded by some as, in fact, the President's lawyer. In the years since it was first established, the office of special counsel has handled many assignments. These have ranged over such areas as speech writing, legislative liaison, development of the administration's legislative program, as well as a number of lawyer chores. These latter include review of congressionally approved bills prior to presidential action, review of airlines overseas route decisions requiring presidential approval, and the like. These legal assignments, along with the very title of the office itself, have caused many an attorney general to wonder if his own status were being whittled away. It has been reported that when President Truman discussed the possibility of appointment as attorney general with a very prominent lawyer, this lawyer asked only one question: would his access to the President be channeled through the office of special counsel or would that office in any sense be a buffer between him and the President? According to the story, the President's answer was in the negative and the attorney promptly accepted the appointment.

Therefore, while a President may involve certain of his staff assistants in dealings with the attorney general he will, by and large, maintain direct personal contact with the attorney general himself. Most Presidents (at least those in recent times) have done this. From the attorney general's point of view, the impulse, indeed the requirement, for direct and clear contact with the President himself is even more pronounced. Several very practical considerations dictate this. As a cabinet officer, the attorney general needs to know the mind of the President. He is the lawyer and the President is his most important client. He is very much like the senior partner of the law firm who lets assistants do much of the support work, but who briefs himself and participates in all conferences with the client. Relationships with the President and the White House are too important to the attorney general to turn them over to assistants. While he may bring an aide or two along, he rarely sends them alone. Also, sensitive to Washington's power structure, no attorney general can permit himself to be moved from his assigned part of the center stage. Such loss of face in Washington would not only be personally unacceptable, but it would also seriously impair the attorney general's ability to function effectively as a member of the President's cabinet.

Therefore, while much may be said and written about the increasingly institutionalized structures of their two offices, the President and the attorney general retain direct contact with one another. To the extent that both are single individuals who sit at the peak of organizational pyramids, personnel within these separate pyramids can, and often do, consult with each other on a routine basis. The contacts are usually informal and highly specialized; and it is here that much routine work gets done.

But if there are many such relationships between the presidency and the Department of Justice, it is equally true that the department in many respects operates autonomously, or with only the slightest of theoretical chains of command leading to the chief executive. The point here may be made in somewhat broader terms: the executive branch of government is not a solid monolith, the component parts of which respond quickly and undeviatingly to presidential command. Because of the sheer weight of numbers and the size and complexity of the tasks for which each of the departments is responsible, necessarily administration must be left to department heads. Broad policy guidelines can be, and are, set by the President, and considerable interplay at the staff level takes place. Nevertheless, the President looks out from the White House, not on a solid front, but on what has been called a collection of "feudalities" made up of the several organizations within the executive branch. Each of these feudalities, including the Department of Justice, has its own drives and interests and, while subject in legal theory to presidential order, are controlled more in theory than in reality. Some effort at control and coordination is made by the Bureau of the Budget, but it remains a fact that the President is not nearly the all-powerful figure within the government many think he is. This does not mean that executive departments and agencies act contrary to express wishes of the President—although there have been instances where they have—but it does mean that they run in large part as autonomous entities. This is true for the Department of Justice as well as for other departments.

This point is illustrated by the political jockeying that took place prior to the passage of the Civil Rights Act of 1957. As documented in Professor Dixon's study (see chapter IV), the act was passed largely through the efforts of Attorney General Herbert Brownell. President Eisenhower favored a bill that would have set up a civil rights commission and created an assistant attorney general for civil rights, and instructed Mr. Brownell to send Congress a bill along these lines. But Attorney General Brownell wanted authority for the Department of Justice to bring suits on behalf of those denied the right to vote and to move in other civil rights matters. By arranging for a friendly congressman (Representative Kenneth Keating, New York) to ask for drafts of bills on the more controversial portions, Brownell was able to get these before Congress. Ultimately, they became part of the Civil Rights Act of 1957. It was not until late in 1956 that the President finally agreed to the stronger bill—after it had passed the House of Representatives!

Action such as that, of course, is rare. It is mentioned here merely to indicate the high degree of autonomy that any cabinet member, including the attorney general, has in running his own department. Admittedly the example is an extreme instance. Nevertheless, it is accurate to say that the executive-administrative branch of the government is far from the monolith that many think it is. As President Harry S Truman said about President-elect Eisenhower in 1952, in discussing the nature of presidential power, "He'll sit here and he'll say, 'Do this! Do that!' *And nothing will happen.* Poor Ike—it won't be a bit like the Army. He'll find it very frustrating." Apparently, President Eisenhower found it so. As Robert Donovan reports: "In the face of continuing dissidence and disunity, the President sometimes simply exploded with exasperation. What was the use, he demanded to know, of his trying to lead the Republican Party. . . ." Professor Richard E. Neustadt, whose book *Presidential Power* is an insightful essay on the presidency, quotes a remark of an Eisenhower aide in 1958: "The President still feels that when he's decided something, that *ought* to be the end of it . . . and when it bounces back undone or done wrong, he tends to react with shocked surprise."

The Department of Justice

To a major extent, as we have seen, the Department of Justice is a self-governing, autonomous entity—dependent, to be sure, upon Congress for funds and its legal basis, and theoretically under the direction of the President. But it is, as are other large government agencies, a collectivity with drives and dynamism of its own.

For the attorney general, himself, the situation is not much different. While he is the operating head of the Department of Justice, it is obvious that he cannot hope to concern himself with the details of its administration. Accordingly, most of his authority under the statutes is delegated to his principal subordinates. These officials, too, have a high degree of autonomy, for routine affairs are entrusted to their administration. While the attorney general may, and does, on special occasion concern himself personally with a matter of detail before one of the sub-offices, normally he is aware of such details only in their broadest form—or when some crisis erupts that requires his attention before it can be resolved.

Accordingly, as in the case of the President, the attorney general is the head of his department in legal theory, but the great bulk of its day-to-day operations, and much of the policymaking, is in the hands of subordinates. As the late Franz Neumann put it, "It is untrue that the decisions of the bureaucrats (public or private) are exclusively routine decisions. Many, indeed, are creative ones, not derived from precedent or standing rules, but highly discretionary and thus essentially lawmaking in character." These policymaking (or lawmaking) activities fit within the broad rubric of presidential desires, or are in accord with the general policy guidelines of the attorney general. Neverthelss, these guidelines at best are broad and nebulous (and sometimes even nonexistent), with the result that much leeway is accorded to subordinates. One example should suffice to make the point. In each of the 50 states (and the District of Columbia) there are United States attorneys who are charged with the responsibility of enforcing federal statutes. While these officers are accountable in theory to the attorney general, in fact, they possess almost complete discretion—for instance, as to whether or not to prosecute a person suspected of crime.

The further point is not that this system is good or bad, but that it is unavoidable—given the size and complexity of the Department of Justice. If the President's power often is more theoretical than real, so far as executive agencies are concerned, so too is the power of the attorney general. This of course is in the nature of any large organization. The same point can be made about large corporations, as the conspiracy cases in the electrical industry illustrate. In those cases, subordinate officers of the General Electric Company and other major electrical firms, entered into collusive agreements with their ostensible competitors—quite without the knowledge, let alone the consent, of the president of G.E.

Politics Collides with Law

The relationship of the attorney general to the President is made more difficult because the attorney general is a *political* officer charged with *legal* duties. He is called upon to render both political and legal advice to the President, as well as legal advice to the other departments of the government. This clash of opposite forces may be seen in the following quotations:

Attorney General Edward Bates (appointed by President Lincoln):

> The office I hold is not properly *political,* but strictly *legal;* and it is my duty, above all other ministers of State to uphold the Law and to resist all encroachments, from whatever quarter, of mere will and power.

Reportedly President Andrew Jackson took the opposite view of the role of the attorney general during the controversy over the national bank in the 1830s. Senator George H. Williams, who was later to become attorney general himself, said many years later:

> Consulting with his Attorney General, he [President Jackson] found that some doubts were entertained by that officer as to the existence of any law authorizing the Executive to do that act [designating certain banks to be depositories of U.S. funds], whereupon Old Hickory said to him, "Sir, you must find a law authorizing the act or I will appoint an Attorney General who will."

Such clashes of polar opposites do not characterize the normal operations of the Department of Justice. The norm is cooperation —between the presidency and the Department of Justice, and between the executive and the legislative. The differences of opinion —the conflicts—get the attention of the press; but these extraordinary occurrences hide and discolor the routine. In short, elements of government must cooperate if the many tasks of government are to be accomplished—and cooperate they do in a routine manner. Nevertheless, when matters of serious public concern occur, the question often arises as to whether a proposed presidential action is in accord with the law. This is as it should be, for the underlying constitutional theory is that this is a "government of laws, and not of men." But stating the theory does not reveal the large degree of discretion which in fact any law officer has in interpreting statutes (and the Constitution) for his superior in the executive branch, whether he be the President, a department head, or some other person within the executive branch.

Furthermore, when providing legal underpinning for proposed executive actions, the attorney may act in a rather different manner from what he would if he were not called upon to find a legal basis for such actions. The President expects his attorney general, it would seem, to be his advocate rather than an impartial arbiter, a judge of the legality of his action. The late Supreme Court Justice Robert H. Jackson, who was both solicitor general and attorney general for President Franklin D. Roosevelt, alluded to the partisan nature of the office in his opinion on President Truman's seizure of the steel mills in 1952. Counsel for the government cited Jackson's position as attorney general in 1941 supporting a seizure of North American Aviation Corporation by President Roosevelt. Referring to his 1941 position, Jackson wrote: "I do not regard it as a precedent for this, but, even if I did, *I should not bind present judicial judgment by earlier partisan advocacy."* (Emphasis added.) It would appear, accordingly, that Mr. Bates' view of the role of the attorney general is less widely accepted than the view attributed to President Jackson. The attorney general is expected to be a partisan.

Perhaps the most revealing account of the close operating contacts between the chief executive and his law officer may be found in the second volume of Francis Biddle's autobiography. Entitled *In Brief Authority,* this book sets out in considerable detail what took place during Mr. Biddle's tenure as attorney general. He held the office during most of the Second World War and thus faced some of the knottiest problems of any such official in American history. Two specific examples, the case of the Nazi saboteurs and the Japanese internment orders, will illustrate what took place.

Shortly after the United States entered World War II, eight Germans were landed secretly at two points on the eastern coast for the purpose of sabotaging, by blowing up war plants, as much of the American war effort as they could. They were captured before any damage was done. The problem then was what to do with them. Clearly they could be incarcerated as prisoners of war. Could the eight be tried *by a military court* for violation of the laws of war, for which the penalty could be death? Some of the men were captured in civilian clothes; while others were in American military uniforms. Did this make them spies and thus subject to trial by court-martial?

As Mr. Biddle recounts it, the American law was somewhat unclear on the matter:

> There was a troublesome Civil War case that seemed to stand in our way. *Ex parte Milligan* . . . decided by the Supreme Court in 1866, at a time when the tide of opinion was running strongly against the excesses indulged in by the Executive while war was being waged—Lincoln, in suppressing rebellion, had not been overtender with civil liberties.

The *Milligan* case has since then (at least until 1942) been considered to stand for the principle that civilians could not be tried by a military court when the civil courts were open and martial law had not been declared. The civil courts *were* open in 1942 and martial law had not been declared. How did this precedent affect the eight Germans?

President Roosevelt, in a memorandum to Biddle, indicated that he thought they should be tried by military court and executed; for two of them he said: "It seems to me that the death penalty is almost obligatory." A special military commission was convened and the men were secretly tried and convicted for offenses against the law of war. They then filed petitions for habeas corpus in federal court, which were denied by the district court and appealed to the United States Supreme Court. The Supreme Court refused to follow the *Milligan* principle and denied habeas corpus. Six of the eight were executed, while the other two were imprisoned because they had "turned state's evidence," that is, had testified as to the plot. Mr. Biddle concludes in this way:

> The defendants had been given every right afforded by our law, and were represented with unusual ability and perseverance by lawyers assigned to them by the country to which they had come in order to wreck war plants. It

was an extraordinary example of justice at its best—prompt, yet fair—in striking contrast to what was going on in Germany.

Two decades later, in a period of sober afterthought, it may be said that the case is not that easy. It has disturbing overtones. One of them underscores the point made above concerning the relationship of the attorney general to the President. The President was determined to have the would-be saboteurs executed. From what we can learn from Mr. Biddle's account, he was equally determined to find a way to accomplish that end. But even more important is the manner in which the Supreme Court, acting hastily (in special session) and without a full bench (only seven justices participated), was made a part of the process. Granted, there are certain actions which must be taken by any head of government during time of war so as to preserve the nation. The term for this is "reason of state" *(raison d'état* or *staatsraison)*. But should these actions be clothed in the familiar garb of legality to which we are accustomed during time of peace? Does this not put law and the legal process, including the federal courts, deeply into politics and thus tend to negate the very idea of law?

The point is a fundamental one and perhaps may be seen more clearly in a second case; the internment of American citizens of Japanese ancestry during World War II. Again, the chief protagonists are the President and his attorney general, and again Mr. Biddle recounts what took place.

When the Japanese navy struck Pearl Harbor in 1941 and catapulted the United States into war, the question soon arose as to what to do with the thousands of aliens of German, Italian, and Japanese nationality (or ancestry). For the Germans and Italians, a selective process of internment was established and some 5,000 in all were confined to special camps set up in North Dakota. But for the Japanese it was a different matter. All the Japanese living in the United States, even those born in this country and thus full American citizens, were removed from the West Coast and incarcerated in internment camps for the duration of the war. Mr. Biddle blames this program on the army and unnamed West Coast politicans, and complains that the "program was expensive and troublesome."

The program troubled him at the time (1942). To him it was

> ... ill-advised, unnecessary, and unnecessarily cruel, taking Japanese who were not suspect, and Japanese Americans whose rights were disregarded, from their homes and from their businesses to sit idly in the lonely misery of barracks while the war was being fought in the world beyond.

But he swallowed his doubts and dutifully went along with an action that has been called "the worst single wholesale violation of civil rights of American citizens in our history." The President and his military leaders wanted the 125,000 Japanese evacuated from the West Coast and penned up. So, the attorney general kept silent, suppressing his earlier views, and the Supreme Court later validated the program. General John L. DeWitt, in command of West Coast military affairs, came to the astounding conclusion that the very fact that there had been no attempts at sabotage by the Japanese-Americans showed an "exercised control," and accordingly that sabotage would have occurred without it! Such "reasoning" provided the basis for the mass incarceration. Although predicated upon military necessity, it is clear—now, and apparently then as well—that no such necessity existed. As J. Edgar Hoover, head of the FBI, said in a memorandum to Mr. Biddle, the evacuation was "based primarily upon public and political pressure rather than on factual data." The Army's historian is in agreement: In 1942, when the evacuation took place, "military estimates of the situation continued to indicate that there was no real threat of a Japanese invasion of the West Coast." No act of espionage or sabotage by the Japanese-Americans ever was proved.

Naturally, since this nation, as we have said, tends to be legalistic and since the Constitution forbids depriving a person of his liberty "without due process of law," cases eventually reached the Supreme Court. The Court upheld the program, in a series of cases which reflect no credit upon it and which prove conclusively that civil liberties can be, and are, sacrificed in time of war. Mr. Biddle concludes in this vein:

> Although the decision has been handed by the President to the Army, and became primarily its responsibility, it is normal to expect the civilian branch of the government to

> have a vision less narrowed to see only the conceivable risks, and to balance against them the seriousness of this basic violation of the civil rights. The President, as I have suggested, was not troubled by such a consideration. If anything, he thought that rights should yield to the necessities of war. Rights came after victory, not before. He could probably have withstood the popular pressure without loss to the tenacity of his leadership—pressure of a highly vocative minority in the West. If Stimson had stood firm, had insisted, as apparently he suspected, that this wholesale evacuation was needless, the President would have followed his advice. And if . . . I had urged the Secretary to resist the pressure of his subordinatism the result might have been different. But I was new to the Cabinet, and disinclined to insist on my view to an elder statesman whose wisdom and integrity I greatly respected.

This plaintive statement from the wartime attorney general reveals the nature of the problem: how to keep the law and the legal process from becoming a tool of political leaders. In the Japanese internment case, the attorney general stepped aside, bowed his head, and said nothing while a wholesale denial of freedom was carried out; in the German saboteur case the attorney general quickly found a legal basis for the President to do what he wanted. And the Supreme Court went along in both instances.

The point here, it is emphasized, is not whether either one of these actions should have been carried out—although as far as the Japanese are concerned a 1959 congressional appropriation indicated a complete change of heart about them. It involves, rather, the question of what should the attorney general do. Should he swallow his conscience and "go along?" Should he resist and, adopting the view of Attorney General Bates, render only "legal" opinions, whatever the consequences? If he does that, he is likely to be bypassed by the President and ignored, while the President relies on other advisers, or (what is more likely) find himself a more pliable attorney general. The attorney general, in other words, can find himself impaled on the horns of a real dilemma, as did Francis Biddle during the World War II Japanese case.

These admittedly are extreme situations, and do not, as noted above, indicate the routine tasks of either the attorney general or the Department of Justice. But by focusing upon the extremes, one is able to discern better the contours of the relationship between the chief executive and his chief law officer.

Another episode illustrating the interplay of law and politics in the office of the attorney general took place a quarter of a century ago. The time was 1940. Europe was at war, the German army had overrun France and forced the English off the continent, and the Battle of Britain was about to begin. In the United States, a major controversy raged over what this country should do. "Isolationism" was at its peak. In 1939, when the war had broken out, the United States had proclaimed its neutrality. However, in 1940 the President and his advisers had deemed it important to the national security that Great Britain be aided in ways short of actually taking sides and declaring war. The British acutely needed additional naval vessels, especially destroyers, for combating the German submarine offensive against ships supplying the British Isles.

Could the President trade 50 American destroyers for long-term leases of military bases on British territory in the western hemisphere? This was the legal question posed to the then attorney general, Robert H. Jackson (later to become an Associate Justice of the Supreme Court). The question was complicated, for it involved three subsidiary questions: (a) Could the President acquire the leases by an executive agreement between himself and the British Prime Minister, or must the agreement be submitted to the Senate as a treaty (and thus subject to possible disapproval by the body)? (b) Did the President have the authority to dispose of the 50 destroyers, and if so, on what conditions? (c) Did the statutes of the United States forbid delivery of such war vessels by reason of the belligerent status of Great Britain? Each of these questions was difficult, but Mr. Jackson was equal to the task. In an opinion rendered August 27, 1940, he answered each in the affirmative—yes, the President could proceed by way of executive agreement and need not submit the agreement to the Senate for its consent; yes, the President does have authority to "alienate the title" to the ships; and yes, the statutes do permit the destroyers to be transferred to Great Britain, even though that nation was at war and even though Congress had enunciated a neutrality policy.

The opinion enabled President Roosevelt to help the British and also to buttress the defenses of the United States in this hemisphere. (Rights to bases acquired under the agreement are still being exercised by this country in several parts of the Caribbean Sea.) In a message to Congress dated September 3, 1940, the President put the urgency of the matter in this way:

> Preparation for defense is an inalienable prerogative of a sovereign state. Under present circumstances this exercise of sovereign right is essential in the maintenance of our peace and safety. This is the most important action in the reinforcement of our national defense that has been taken since the Louisiana Purchase. Then as now, considerations of safety from overseas attack were fundamental.
>
> The value to the Western Hemisphere of these outposts of security is beyond calculation.

The decision raised considerable controversy at the time. Some legal scholars asserted that the attorney general's opinion was faulty, and that he had unduly stretched the law in order to accommodate it to the wishes of the President. As Professor Herbert W. Briggs of Cornell University put it:

> The destroyers have by now been transferred; but let no one say that it was accomplished "legally." The supplying of these vessels by the United States Government to a belligerent is a violation of our neutral status, a violation of our national law, and a violation of international law.

While others in the academic world disagreed with Professor Briggs and sided with the attorney general, it is fair to say that a respectable body of opinion in the United States thought that the attorney general had gone too far in accommodating law to the exigencies of politics. (The term "politics" is not used here in any invidious sense, but rather to denote the decisions of political leaders, who, as noted above, believed that the requirements of national security made it essential that the agreement with Great Britain be consummated.) Without taking sides on the question of legality, the case does reveal the extremes to which the President's chief law officer can be pushed. For had Mr. Jackson not produced an opinion validating the agreement, it is possible that the President would have found a new attorney general more pliable to his wishes. As has been previously mentioned, a few years later Attorney General Francis Biddle had to bury his conscience and suppress sticky legal questions about the forced evacuation and internment of Japanese-Americans.

The destroyer opinion raises crucial constitutional questions and is an illustration of how a President calls upon his law officer for aid in furthering what he, the President, deems necessary. This instance involved urgent matters of national security, and thus reveals some of the powers the chief executive has exercised during periods of international tension. A somewhat analogous situation occurred in 1962, in the famous "eyeball-to-eyeball" encounter between the United States and the Soviet Union over Russian missiles in Cuba. Again, the President was determined to take action, and this time, the question was whether Soviet ships bearing arms to Cuba could be stopped and searched. Normally a blockade is considered an act of war. However, could the ship searches be called a "quarantine" and thus be a lawful measure of self-defense short of war? The issue became acute midway in the tense period of several days when the confrontation took place. There was no time, however, to have an attorney general's formal opinion researched and written. Accordingly, lawyers from the State Department met with the deputy attorney general and others from the Department of Justice; after a few hours of discussion, a draft opinion was produced which maintained that the United States could quarantine Cuba and that this action was not an "act of war" under international law. The President proceeded on this basis, and the matter was settled a few days later when the USSR backed down. Here, again, grave questions of constitutional and international law were involved; here, again, the attorney general was able, under the most adverse circumstances, to help produce a viable legal document to legalize what the President wanted to do.

And here, again, it may be said, the idea of the law as a normative, nay-saying body of principles that could interdict proposed presidential actions gave way to the harsh realities of power politics —to *realpolitik*. Law, in these cases, became a purposive instrument of action, and the lawyer's task was not to say "no" but to find a way to say "yes." (This recalls the perhaps apocryphal statement of a high military officer during the Second World War: "I don't want eighteen lawyers around telling me what I cannot do; what I want is one lawyer telling me that I can do what is necessary.") In doing this, the lawyer was not advising the President as to the wisdom of proposed action; instead, he was saying that if the President considered a given action to be necessary, a legal basis was present. This point may be seen in a request by President Abraham Lincoln to Attorney General Edward Bates, and in that officer's reply. The President asked whether he could legally and *should* provision Fort Sumter. Mr. Bates replied: "This is not a question of lawful right, but of prudence and patriotism only." It was, in other words, both a military and a political matter, and the attorney general did not deem himself competent to advise on such matters. "As a counselor of the President," Bates wrote in his diary, "I do not presumptuously set myself up as a commander." (It should be noted that the American people, speaking generally, care far less for what are often called "mere technicalities" than do lawyers. As the biographer of Robert H. Jackson has noted, President Roosevelt's trade of destroyers for bases made sense to the people generally. It was only certain legal scholars who raised uncomfortable questions of legality. Thus, the American people, although legalistic in nature, at times are quite impatient about the technicalities of law.)

Not all attorneys general, as we have seen, have been able to divorce themselves from the heat of politics as neatly as Mr. Bates. In fact, it seems to be a fair generalization to say that the attorney general is enmeshed in the administration. In his advisory capacity to the President who must "take care that the laws be faithfully executed," the government's chief legal officer is drawn increasingly into the political arena. We have noted the examples of Attorneys General Jackson, Biddle, and Brownell. Another instance can be found in the recent, greatly increased activity of the Department of Justice in the field of civil rights, particularly with reference to the position of the Negro in American society. Since the Supreme Court's decision in 1938 in the *Missouri Law School Case*—the decision which began the erasure of "separate but equal" from the nation's public schools—the Department of Justice has intervened on an accelerating scale in civil rights cases. This drive, which is discussed in another chapter, took on added speed after the Supreme Court outlawed "separate but equal" in the famous *Brown* decision in 1954. And as we have seen, the Civil Rights Act of 1957 put the Department of Justice (and the attorney general) in the middle of this country's most pressing and politically sensitive internal problem. The Civil Rights Act of 1964, it may be noted, gave the Department of Justice important new responsibilities in this field.

Accordingly, many of the attorney general's decisions, although of a legal nature, have had great political impact. Such decisions run all the way from the use of the FBI to the prosecution of alleged deprivations of civil rights. Also, there is little opportunity for an attorney general to take the aloof posture of Edward Bates. The proliferation of federal statutes, many of which the Department of Justice is charged with enforcing, means that the department is in politics and probably will remain there.

What is involved is the enforcement of the law, the law as enunciated in the form of statutes enacted by Congress, the law as articulated by the United States Supreme Court in its constitutional decision-making process, and the law as announced by the President in his independent capacity. Despite the myth to the contrary—a myth which at times has had the high sanction of the Supreme Court itself—the lawmaking proclivities of the federal government are not limited to Congress. And laws, once promulgated, must be enforced—and it is here that the attorney general and his 31,-000-plus associates come into action.

Law Enforcement

Enforcement of the law ultimately means calling into operation the power of a court, criminal or civil. Congress has made the Department of Justice the principal organ entrusted with this fundamental function. Under the terms of the United States Code (Title 5, Section 49), "No head of a department shall employ attorneys or counsel at the expense of the United States; but when in need of counsel or advice, shall call upon the Department of Justice, the officers of which shall attend to the same. . . ." This, it may be noted, should not be taken literally. What it refers to is counsel in government *litigation;* as we have noted above, there are far more lawyers *outside* the Department of Justice than within it.

If enforcement means litigation—taking someone to court—and if the Department of Justice is the focal point of all government litigation, then it is also true that within the department exists one office with a specialized function which may be used to indicate the flow and sweep of the work in court. As has been noted above, the attorney general as the chief law officer of the government is primarily an administrator and a presidential adviser. Congress has provided for another officer, the solicitor general, who also must be a person "learned in the law." It is the solicitor general, and his small coterie of lawyers, who functions under the attorney general as the highest government official engaged solely in litigation.

Many distinguished lawyers have filled the office; to name but a few: John W. Davis, William D. Mitchell, Stanley Reed, Robert H. Jackson, Francis Biddle, and Charles Fahy. The work of the solicitor general's office, which may be said to encompass the highest quality legal work in the government, includes the following:

(a) The staff, made up of not more than a dozen carefully selected lawyers, reviews the briefs prepared by lawyers elsewhere in the government on cases appealed from a lower court's decision. The original briefs are drafted in other divisions of the Department of Justice or in one of the other agencies (such as the National Labor Relations Board, the Securities and Exchange Commission, etc.). But all are reviewed, and usually rewritten, in the office of the solicitor general. These briefs then become the written presentations in appellate court.

Whether and to what extent the solicitor general himself reads the briefs varies with the person in the office. He will of course read those in all important cases and those which he personally argues in court. Some solicitors general have read all briefs that passed through the office; others have relied more heavily on their staffs.

(b) The second principal activity is oral argument in court. The government is a party in some way in about 60 percent of the cases argued in the Supreme Court; this means that the solicitor general's office is responsible for about 60 to 90 arguments each year. The solicitor general assigns all of the government's oral presentations before the Supreme Court. Some he may take himself, generally the most important ones. Others are distributed to his staff or to attorneys in the Department of Justice. Still others may go to attorneys in other government agencies.

(c) The solicitor general decides which cases the government can appeal, as well as assigning attorneys for oral argument. Except for the Interstate Commerce Commission and in certain other instances, no appeal can be taken to the courts of appeal or to the United States Supreme Court without the solicitor general's permission. For that matter, there can be no decision not to appeal a lower court's decision without his approval. It is true that the litigation at trial court level (the federal district courts, located in every state) is in the control of the agencies themslves or of the federal district attorneys in each state. But once a case has been decided in that court, the solicitor general is in command. These cases, it should be noted, are those in which the government is a party or has an interest (such as being an amicus curiae, discussed elsewhere in this book).

In deciding whether or not an appeal should be taken, as well as in reviewing the briefs drafted in other offices, the lawyers in the solicitor general's office necessarily work closely with their colleagues in other offices of the department. The norm is cooperation, but fairly often conflicts occur, particularly when the solicitor general refuses to approve a case for appeal. Such differences of opinion often flow from the fact that the solicitor general considers himself—and the Supreme Court regards him—as both an officer of the executive branch and an officer of the Court. Former Solicitor General (now Judge) Simon Sobeloff summed up this feature in the following words:

> The Solicitor General is not a neutral, he is an advocate; but an advocate whose business is not merely to prevail in the instant case. My client's chief business is not to achieve victory, but to establish justice. We are constantly reminded of the now classic words penned by one of my illustrious predecessors, Frederick William Leh-

mann, that the Government wins its point when justice is done in the courts.

The zeal of the advocate, often reflected in the lawyers who work for other government agencies, must at times be tempered by the broader interests of the solicitor general.

Sometimes this leads the solicitor general to an unusual position —that of "confessing error" in the Supreme Court. If he believes that the position the government took in the lower court to be completely untenable, he will so advise the Supreme Court—and thus in effect request that Court to rule against his client! Confessions of error occur when the government has won its case below, and the other party has appealed. (If the government lost in the district court, and wants to appeal, there need be no confession of error. All the solicitor general has to do—in instances where he considers the government's case to be unworthy—is to refuse to permit the appeal.) But it is a relative rarity for the solicitor general to confess error; the usual thing is to go along. As Robert L. Stern, who served many years in the office, has said:

> Whether or not error should be confessed or an agency not supported usually does not present a simple problem. The Solicitor General is aware that to confess error will not only infuriate the attorneys who have handled the case for the Government below, but also the judges who were persuaded to decide in the Government's favor. . . .

Thus the solicitor general must do considerable soul-searching before he reverses the government's position. It is not sufficient that he believes the government may lose on appeal. He must also believe there is no respectable argument on the government's side.

Centralizing control over the government's appellate litigation in this manner has produced a number of benefits. In the first place, the quality of the briefs and arguments is often greatly improved. This does not mean that capable lawyers do not exist elsewhere in the government, but merely that a fresh mind coming at a problem can provide considerable help. Secondly, the lawyer in the solicitor general's office usually takes a broader view than does the lawyer in another agency. The solicitor general and his staff are used to seeing matters in a wider perspective and with greater objectivity than do those who are enmeshed in the daily routine of one specialized office. Thirdly, the solicitor general is in a better position to comply with Supreme Court's standards in the handling of litigation. And finally, by centralizing appellate litigation, better coordination of governmental policy is effected. The federal government is so large that sometimes one agency will pursue a policy or take a position contrary to that of another. One way, although not the only way, that consistency in policy can be maintained is through control of appellate litigation, particularly in the Supreme Court.

But appellate court work is not the only side of the law enforcement picture. The attorney general also administers two other very important facets of enforcement: police work and prosecution. Both merit some mention. Police work is in the hands of the Federal Bureau of Investigation. Headed by Mr. J. Edgar Hoover, this largely autonomous office within the Department of Justice has over 14,000 employees. Law enforcement in the United States, speaking broadly, is a responsibility of the state governments; there is, as the saying goes, no "national police force." Nevertheless the proliferation of the federal government during this century has been accompanied by the enactment of literally dozens of statutes assigning new responsibilities to the FBI. And, as a result, something akin to a national police force seems to be either in being or in the making.

These statutes involve a wide variety of different problems—ranging in importance from anti-Communist activity through organized crime to investigations of fraud against the government and theft of government property. In the criminal area, they include racketeering, labor-management and antitrust laws and regulations, assaulting or killing a federal officer, bank robberies, bribery and conflict of interest among government employees, crimes aboard aircraft and on the high seas, crimes on government and Indian reservations, embezzlement in Federal Reserve banks, extortion and kidnapping, federal housing administration matters, illegal wearing of military uniforms, impersonation of federal officers, and interstate gambling. In addition, the FBI undertakes hundreds of civil investigations dealing with contract matters and other claims against the government. It also cooperates closely with local enforcement officials.

What is in the making is a true national police force. As federal activity expands, so too does the work of the Department of Justice —and of the FBI. Congress has deemed it necessary to deal with crimes committed in interstate commerce and otherwise to reach down and assert federal responsibility over matters traditionally local in nature. The movement seems to be increasing. At some time, therefore, the FBI will be recognized as a national police force—in fact, if not in theory. (This, it may be noted, is not to place a normative judgment on the matter. The combination of new technology, which has greatly speeded communications and transportation, and the fact that American business corporations now operate nationwide in a true American "common market," has made such a development almost inevitable.)

The FBI investigates. The federal district attorneys (or special attorneys from the Department of Justice) prosecute, both in criminal and in civil cases. These officials, who are located in every state (some states have more than one such office), are vested with discretionary responsibility over enforcement through the courts of most of the thousands of cases occurring yearly in which the government is involved. Most—almost all—of this very important activity does not get presidential attention. Nor, for that matter, does it receive the attention of the attorney general or of officials in the Department of Justice in Washington. The federal district attorneys operate in a largely discretionary manner. In fact, it is not unknown for some of them either to ignore or to dispute any attempted direction from Washington.

The President and Congress

The attorney general performs a specialized function for the President with respect to Congress. This function involves comment on proposed legislation that comes within the ambit of the department's responsibility as well as advice on the legal meaning to be given to certain legislative actions. One area merits special attention, for it illustrates an evolution in congressional-presidential relations: the growing tendency of Congress to try to control the details of administration.

The situation emanates from the growth of the "administrative state"—the system whereby Congress has established a number of administrative agencies and government departments and invested them with authority to do certain acts. Often these delegations of authority from Congress are accompanied by the loosest of standards. The agency or commission or department is charged with regulating "in the public interest" or, to take the case of the Federal Communications Commission, as "the public convenience, interest, or necessity requires. . . ." The result of such delegations has been the cession of discretionary power to the delegate to set his own standards and indeed in some cases to act without any standards at all. It has led such observers as federal Judge Henry J. Friendly to issue a call for "better definition of standards" by administrators. But his call has not yet been answered.

Congress, having ceded authority over large segments of what it considers to be its rightful responsibility, has been searching for means to retain its power as a coordinate branch of government without unduly interfering with the public administration. Two techniques are employed: (a) an informal technique which allows the chairmen of the major standing committees of Congress, who have long tenure under the seniority system, to exercise much actual power over the way in which laws are in fact executed by the executive branch; and (b) a formal technique, sometimes called "coming into agreement," which requires that certain proposed administrative decisions be referred to appropriate congressional committees for designated periods (often 60 days) and which permits the committees to approve or disapprove those decisions. It is the latter device which is of interest here.

The attorney general takes part in advising the President as to the legality of such attempts by Congress to participate in administration. Two examples, one by President Lyndon B. Johnson and the other by President Franklin D. Roosevelt, will illustrate the question. In December, 1963, Congress enacted the Public Works Appropriation bill, one provision of which stated that the Panama Canal Company was precluded from disposing of real property without first obtaining the approval of the appropriate committees of the House and Senate. President Johnson signed the bill, but in a statement issued on December 31, 1963, he had this to say concerning that provision:

> Four Attorneys General of the United States have held provisions of this nature unconstitutional. The opinions of the Attorneys General point out that it is either an unconstitutional delegation to Congressional committees of powers which reside only in the Congress as a whole, or an attempt to confer executive powers on the committees in violation of the principle of separation of powers set forth in the Constitution.
>
> I concur in these views.
>
> However, it is entirely proper for the committees to request information with respect to the disposal of property, and I recognize the desirability of consultations between officials of the Executive Branch and the Congress. Therefore, it is my intention to treat the provision as a request for information and to direct that the appropriate legislative committees be kept fully informed with respect to the disposal and transfer actions taken by the Panama Canal Company.

Here, again, is an instance of the attorney general advising the President as to his constitutional powers. It differs from those discussed above, however, in that it deals with the delicate relationships between President and Congress. Such opinions as these are, of course, normally not written by the attorney general himself; and it may be that he may have had only a cursory acquaintance with this particular attempt of Congress to retain control over the details of administration. Opinions on matters such as these usually originate in the Office of Legal Counsel, headed by an assistant attorney general. But ultimately the attorney general signs them and takes responsibility, even though he may not be aware of their content.

The other example, to be contrasted with the action taken by President Johnson, is noteworthy for a special reason: it is the only known instance in which a President rendered a legal opinion to the attorney general. The facts are these: Congress passed the Lend-Lease Act in 1941. This statute was designed to aid friendly nations in World War II, through the transfer of munitions and war materials. One provision read as follows:

After June 30, 1943, or after the passage of a concurrent resolution of the two Houses before June 30, 1943, which declares that the powers conferred by or pursuant to subsection (a) are no longer necessary to promote the defense of the United States, neither the President nor the head of any department or agency shall exercise any of the powers conferred by or pursuant to subsection (a).

The President thought this provision unconstitutional, because it permitted Congress to repeal legislation by concurrent resolution, which is not subject to the President's constitutional power of veto. Nevertheless, he signed the bill, because "the emergency was so great." A few days later, in order to put his doubts about the constitutionality of the provision on record, he signed a memorandum to the attorney general (which, it may be noted, had been prepared by an assistant to the attorney general) in which he set forth his reasons for approving the bill even though it contained the objectionable clause. The President wished to make sure his approval would not be construed as a tacit acquiescence in the provision and would not be used "as a precedent for any future legislation comprising provisions of a similar nature." And he asked Attorney General Jackson to keep the memorandum and publish it at a later suitable date. President Roosevelt concluded this extraordinary memorandum with a quote from President Andrew Jackson: "I deem it an imperative duty to maintain the supremacy of that sacred instrument (the Constitution) and the immunities of the Department entrusted to my care."

What is involved here is attempted control over the details of public administration by the Congress. One may note the two techniques employed in the different examples cited. For President Johnson, it involved the Army's "coming into agreement" with the appropriate congressional committees. For President Roosevelt, it was a question of whether Congress could eliminate his power of veto. In both instances the attorney general played an important role. Thus may be seen the impact of the attorney general and the Department of Justice in the continuing intramural jousting for power between Congress and the President. Although the attorney general and all of the employees of the department are dependent upon Congress for both the legal basis of their existence and the appropriations to permit them to operate, nevertheless their loyalties flow toward the President. They are members of the executive branch, itself equal in constitutional dignity to the Congress and they act as such. This is not to say, however, that the attorney general is immune from congressional control. As pointed out in chapter I, on two occasions the Congress has enacted legislation taking important cases out of the control of the attorney general and placing them in charge of special counsel.[2] In other cases the Congress has appointed special counsel when the position of the President was at odds with the position of the Congress.[3]

Conclusion

This chapter has been a rather impressionistic view of the relationships between the attorney general and the President. We have seen that each of those officials should be viewed as an organization, as well as an individual. This means that there is a complex web of interactions between the Department of Justice and the presidency, the great bulk of which never receive public attention. In addition, the attorney general is both a political and a legal officer. This dual capacity creates situations of tension in which he must make judgments as to how far the law and the legal system may be employed to meet the desires of the chief executive.

---

[2] 43 Stat. at L. 5, 15, 16.
[3] See, for example, Lovett et al., 328 U.S. 303.

III.

THE ROLE OF THE ATTORNEY GENERAL AS AMICUS CURIAE

By Samuel Krislov

A Friend of the Court—The Traditional Concept

THE TERM amicus curiae has become commonplace in our legal literature. But its origin and evolution, as well as its involvement in the role of the attorney general, have been largely ignored. Literally, of course, it means "a friend of the court" and it ordinarily implies the friendly intervention of counsel to aid the court.[1] According to Abbott's Dictionary of Words and Phrases, amicus curiae means:

> ... a bystander, who without having an interest in the cause ... makes suggestions on a point of law or of fact for the information of the presiding judge.

As explained in a legal dictionary of older vintage,

> Counsel in court frequently act in this capacity when they happen to be in possession of a case which the judge has not seen or does not at the moment remember.[2]

---
[1] 4 Am Jur 2d, *Amicus Curiae*, § 1.
[2] Holthouse's Law Dictionary.

As suggested by these definitions, the concept of amicus curiae developed in England at a time when modern law reporter systems were unknown and the enactments of Parliament were slow in reaching the local courts. In early English practice, precedents and statutes were sometimes recited from memory and, indeed, amicus curiae "was permitted to state in court that he was present at the making of a statute and what was the intention of Parliament in enacting the law."[3] In one case a member of Parliament appeared as amicus curiae and informed the court of the intent of a particular law.[4] As the common law evolved, the aid of disinterested members of the bar was warmly received because it was "for the honour of the courts to avoid error in their judgments."[5]

Under Roman law, the presiding judge could invite or appoint an attorney to act as *consiliarius*—that is, assistant judge—to enlighten the court on points of law.[6] In early English law, any attorney could volunteer as amicus curiae and offer advice without invitation from or appointment by the court.[7] In modern practice in the United States a court may appoint amicus curiae, or grant him leave to appear on his own application.

Third Party Interests Under the Common Law of England

The common law courts[8] strongly resisted partisan participation by counsel for third parties—parties not entitled to participate as plaintiff or defendant. But there were some departures where the outcome of a case might directly affect the rights of an outsider. For example, in the case of *Coxe* v. *Phillips*,[9] decided in 1736, Mr. Coxe sued Mrs. Phillips to collect on a promissory note. Mrs. Phillips defended on the ground that at the time the note was signed she was married to one Muilman and that as a married woman she

---

[3] 4 Am Jur 2d, Amicus Curiae, § 3, note 18, citing Haley v. Eureka County Bank, 21 Nev. 127, 26 p. 64.
[4] Harton & Ruesby, Comb. 33, 90 Eng. Rep. 326 (K.B. 1686).
[5] The Protector v. Geering, 145 Eng. Rep. 394 (Ex. 1656).
[6] See Wenger, *Institutes on the Roman Law of Civil Procedure* 202 (Rev. Ed. 1940); Jolowicz, *Historical Introduction to Roman Law* 92 (1932).
[7] See The Prince's Case & Co. 13b, 77 Eng. Rep. 496 (Ch. 1609), wherein an appearance was made "ut amici curiae and to inform the Court of the Truth."
[8] The courts under the common law of England prior to the American Revolution.
[9] 95 Eng. Rep. 152 (K.B. 1736).

was without legal capacity to enter into a binding contract. But her marriage to Muilman had been annulled and he had remarried. Muilman was permitted to have his interests represented by counsel in the role of amicus curiae. By this procedure he was successful in protecting his reputation and in having the defendant held in contempt of court. The significance of this case, of course, is that Muilman's counsel appeared both as amicus curiae and as an advocate for a person who was not a party to the law suit. Thus, a step was taken toward changing the role of amicus curiae from neutrality to advocacy. It should be emphasized, however, that in the *Coxe* case amicus curiae advocated his own interests—not the interests of the plaintiff or defendant.

Traditional Limitations on the Role of Amicus Curiae in the United States

Although there were some notable exceptions, the concept that amicus curiae "acts for no one, but simply seeks to give information to the court" [10] seems to have been the general rule in the United States for many years. In fact, it appears that the amicus curiae procedure was not used in the Supreme Court until a rare situation arose in 1821.

The question of whether counsel shall be granted permission to participate as amicus curiae has always been a matter within the discretion of the courts and for this reason decisions on the questions have not been regarded as having great precedential value. Accordingly, even at the federal level references to the role of amicus curiae are sketchy and some of the rulings governing amicus curiae are difficult to reconcile. The Supreme Court of the United States did not mention amicus curiae in its written rules of procedure until 1937 and the federal courts generally have avoided a precise definition of the circumstances under which the amicus curiae device could be used.[11] It is of interest, however, to compare the limited role of amicus curiae as viewed by various state and federal courts in some cases in earlier years with the subsequent view of the Department of Justice and the Supreme Court of the United States. Decisions that

---

[10] Campbell v. Swasey, 12 Ind. 70, 72 (1859).
[11] The Congress has never formulated a definition and in the absence of legislation, the matter has been left to "the inherent power of a court of law to control its processes." Krippendorf v. Hyde, 110 U.S. 276, 283 (1884).

have tended to expand the role of amicus curiae and the current practice in the Supreme Court are discussed later in this chapter.

It has been held that amicus curiae has no right to participate as a formal party;[12] may not participate unless he is involved in other litigation that might be affected by the outcome of the case;[13] cannot assume the functions of a partisan;[14] has no control over the litigation;[15] may not raise an issue not raised by the parties to an action;[16] may not inject a new issue on appeal that was not before the trial court;[17] and, finally, may not move for dismissal of an action.[18] As late as 1950 a distinguished jurist asserted that "the parties to a controversy should have the right to litigate the same free from the interference of strangers." [19]

Expansion of the Role of Amicus Curiae— the Shift From Neutrality to Partisanship

Amicus Curiae as an Advocate of Private Interests. As the role of government and the federal courts expanded, so did pressures to expand the role of amici curiae. Spokesmen for private as well as government interests found it difficult to intervene under the rules governing participation in litigation as a "party." [20] As a result the courts began to gradually expand the role of amicus curiae. At times as intervenors, at times as amicus curiae, depending on the situation and requests of the litigants or agreements of the counsel, private litigants of similar cases pending before the lower courts and parties to lower court proceedings in a case before the Supreme Court who had not joined in the appeal were allowed to state their

---

[12] Glenel Realty Corp. v. Worthington (Sup) 161 NYS2d 777.
[13] Northern Securities Co. v. United States, 191 US 555, 48 L ed 299, 24 S Ct 119.
[14] Re Ohlhauser's Estate (SD) 101 NW2d 827.
[15] Birmingham Loan & Auction Co. v. First Nat. Bank, 100 Ala. 249, 13 So 945; State v. McDonald, 63 Or 467, 128 P 835; Re McClellan, 27 SD 109, 129 NW 1037.
An amicus curiae is not vested with the management of the case. Hyde Corp v. Huffines, 158 Tex 566, 3134 SW2d 763,*cert. denied,*358 U.S. 898, 3 L ed 2d 148, 79 S Ct 223.
[16] Kemp v. Rubin, 187 Misc 707, 64 NYS2d 510. He may not introduce new issues; only the issues raised by the parties may be considered. Dawes v. Silberman, 185 Misc 335, 56 NYS2d 902.
[17] Robertson v. Hert's Admr. 312 Ky 405, 227 SW2d 899.
[18] State v. McDonald, 63 Or 467, 128 P 835; Re McClellan, 27 SD 109, 129 NW 1037.
[19] See Frank, *Courts on Trial,* 80-102 (1950).
[20] For explanation of rules on intervention as a formal party, see p. 88.

views by brief or oral presentation. Others claiming to be "real parties" in the case, or persons who could be directly injured by a decision, were sometimes extended similar privileges.

As our judicial system developed certain types of litigation raised complex questions regarding the number of participants.[21] Patent suits between the licensee and other parties often involved the holders of the patent; land and admiralty cases raised similar issues. Tax cases[22] and cases involving Indians and their rights[23] presented a variety of problems of representation. In a somewhat tardy fashion, the evolving use of the amicus brief as a form of third party representation came to be reflected in the nomenclature.

Formerly, the amicus curiae stood in an essentially professional relation to the Court and it was the lawyer himself, rather than any organization that was regarded as the amicus. Throughout the last half of the nineteenth century the Supreme Court clung to this approach. Since then, and apparently without self-consciousness, the neutral role of amicus curiae has been totally forgotten. By the 1930s, the open identification of amicus brief with an organizational sponsor was quite commonplace.[24]

The attribution of a brief to an organization belies the traditional lawyer-like role of the amicus. However, it realistically embraces and ratifies the transformation of the amicus from a neutral, amorphous embodiment of justice, into an active participant in the interest group struggle.

In cases where the stakes for interest groups are high, and where the judges needs for information and for the sharing of responsibility through consultation are at a peak, access has appropriately, and almost inevitably, been at its greatest. Occasionally state courts refuse briefs by "friends of the court" for being "excessively partisan,"[25] or because a party "is acting (though under disguise) not as a friend of the court but as a friend of one of the contestant

---

[21] See, e.g., Bate Refrig. Co. v. Hammond, 129 U.S. 151 (1889); White-Smith Music Co. v. Appollo Co., 209 U.S. 1 (1908), and the discussion in Northern Security Co. v. United States, 191 U.S. 555 (1903).

[22] See, e.g., Strattons Independence Ltd. v. Collector, 231 U.S. 399 (1913).

[23] See, e.g., Wallace v. Adams, 204 U.S. 415 (1907).

[24] See, e.g., United States v. Butler, 297 U.S. 1 (1935).

[25] First Citizens Bank & Trust Co. v. Saranac, 243 App. Div. 843, 278 N.Y.S. 203, *aff'd*, 246 App. Div. 672, 283 N.Y.S. 498 (1935).

litigants before said court." [26] However, the Supreme Court of the United States makes no pretense of such disinterestedness on the part of "its friends." [27] It treats the amicus as a potential litigant in future cases, as an ally of one of the parties, or as the representative of an interest not otherwise represented. At this level, then, the transition in the role of the amicus curiae is complete; at lower court levels it is still in process.

Amicus Curiae as an Advocate of Governmental Interests. Where obvious injustice would be caused by lack of representation the courts have always allowed outsiders to intervene. Generally this has been done by exercise of what was called "the inherent power of a court of law to control its processes." [28] No great ceremony was attendant on this; often the court merely extended the privilege of filing a brief "by leave of the court." Gradually this practice came to be controlled by a set of increasingly formal rules that were communicated more or less informally to the regular practitioners before the Court, or those who habitually handled similar cases on other levels. It was only at a much later date that some of these rules were codified

As the Supreme Court approached the era of semi-political decisions, a number of third party devices other than amicus curiae were at hand. "The ways of the third party" developed by the courts in this field range widely in degrees of formality. A list suggested in the late 1920s included among others: (a) leave to intervene as a party or a quasi-party (the right to intervene *as a party* has become more general, particularly in the twentieth century and is based in part upon legislation); (b) participation as an ancillary party; (c) petition or motion or presentation of claim on a fund; (d) suggestion or memo; (e) special appearance; (f) class suits.[29]

Further, in less rigorously legalistic days, when the attorney general was permitted by law and indeed forced by circumstance to maintain a private practice, it was often possible for him to serve two masters in a case. Sometimes he could advance the position of "the United States" by merely acting as counsel for a party; this seems

---

[26] Brief for Respondent, p. 59, City of Grand Rapids v. Consumers Power Co., 216 Mich. 409, 185 N.W. 852 (1921).
[27] See Universal Oil Products Co. v. Root Refrigerating Co., 328 U.S. 575 (1946).
[28] Krippendorf v. Hyde, 110 U.S. 276, 283 (1884).
[29] Hersman, "Intervention in Federal Courts," 61 *Am. L. Rev.* 1, 4-6 (1927).

to have been the case, for example, in *Gibbons* v. *Ogden*.[30] In other instances he might represent both the interest of the government and obtain a fee for private activity as well. The early usages of the third party devices tended to be of these more informal sorts.

In *Hayburn's Case*[31] in 1792, Randolph was not allowed to move "ex officio" for the government, because the Court "entertained great doubt upon his right . . . to proceed" in this manner. He then changed his status to private counsel and argued the case for Hayburn. Another mode which emerged through the years by which third parties were permitted to participate was the "suggestion" or "general courtesy," as in the case of *The Schooner Exchange*.[32] More formally, in 1821, Pinckney was heard upon the application of "the executive" in the case of *The Amiable Isabella*.[33] As the headnote of this case suggests, accommodation of broader interests was commencing in formal fashion, for the reporter states that "where a case involved the construction of a treaty, the court heard a third argument on the application of the *executive government* of the United States."[34] In any event, all of these modes of representation merge into one another, and in various epochs have often been functional equivalents.

Even in recent years, the precise standing of a party may often be somewhat vague and differently interpreted by the parties and commentators; the line between an intervenor (a party) and amicus curiae is often blurred. In former years the lines were even vaguer, and contradictions and anomalies were quite common.

In the celebrated case of *Green* v. *Biddle*[35] a decision relating to land holdings in Kentucky was made by the Supreme Court without any representation on the part of that state. Under instructions from the State of Kentucky, Henry Clay made an appearance as an amicus curiae and sought a rehearing. On March 12, 1821, Clay—

---

[30] 22 U.S. (9 Wheat.) 1 (1824). See Klonoski, The Influence of Government Counsel on Supreme Court Decisions Involving the Commerce Power 1, 10, 10 n.3, 12 (Ann Arbor: University Microfilms) (1958).
[31] Hayburn's Case, 2 U.S. (2 Dallas) 408 (1792).
[32] 11 U.S. (7 Cranch.) 116 (1812).
[33] The Amiable Isabella, 19 U.S. (6 Wheat.) 1, 50 (1821).
[34] *Id.* at 50. Emphasis added. Similarly, in United States v. The Late Corporation of the Church of Jesus Christ of Latterday Saints, 150 U.S. 145 (1893), *"Mr. Solicitor General* watched the case on behalf of the United States."
[35] 21 U.S. (8 Wheat.) 1 (1823).

> . . . as amicus curiae moved for a rehearing in the cause, upon the ground that it involved the rights and claims of numerous occupants of the land. . . . He stated, that the rights and interests of those claimants would be irrevocably determined by this decision of the court, the tenant in the present cause having permitted it to be brought to a hearing, without appearing by counsel, and without any argument on that side of the question.[36]

Faced with behavior on the part of one of the nominal participants that strongly suggested collusion, the Court allowed the extraordinary procedure and granted the plea for a rehearing on petition of an amicus curiae.[37] Amicus curiae had never been deemed to be a "party," and had never been allowed to initiate such an important procedural motion. But Clay, acting as amicus curiae, was permitted to do so and to argue the case. In view of the prevailing attitude that "an amicus curiae cannot perform any act on behalf of a party," that "he acts for no one," this debut of the amicus curiae in the Supreme Court must be recognized as a dramatic and unusual one.[38]

The next major step[39] in the development of amicus curiae occurred in 1854 when the Supreme Court was forced, in *Florida* v. *Georgia*,[40] to articulate some of the factors involved in such participation. In that case, the request of the United States' attorney general to be heard was opposed by counsel for the two states, and the Court was forced to grant or deny permission on its own initiative. Defining the problem, Chief Justice Taney noted that "it is the familiar practice of the Court to hear the Attorney General in suits between

---

[36] 21 U.S. at 17.
[37] Green v. Biddle, 21 U.S. (8 Wheat.) 1, 17 (1823).
[38] See 35 Am. & Eng. Ann. Cas. 193-98 (1915A); compare Green v. Biddle, 21 U.S. (8, Wheat.), 1, 17 (1823) *with* Campbell v. Swasey, 12 Ind. 70 (1859).
[39] There were prior conventional uses of amicus curiae. In *Ex parte* Randolph, 20 Fed. Cas. 242 (No. 11,558) (C.C. Va. 1833), a representative of the United States appeared, stating specifically that "he appeared in the case at the request of the court, as amicus curiae, and did not feel himself at liberty to make any admissions." *Id.* at 244. He did, however, venture the opinion in passing that "it was the fashion of the times, to raise constitutional questions, and nullify acts of congress." *Id.* at 250. And in Lord v. Veazie, 49 U.S. (8 How.) 250 (1850), the Taney Court allowed a suggestion by amicus curiae, and agreed that the suit was collusive. See also, *In re* Ah Yup, 1 Fed. Cas. 223 (No. 104) (C.C. Cal. 1878), where the entire Bar was invited to make "such suggestions as amicus curiae as occurred to them." *Ibid.*
[40] 58 U.S. (17 How.) 478 (1854).

individuals, when he suggests that the public interests are involved . . . not as counsel for one of the parties . . . but on behalf of the United States."[41]

In the decades that followed, the amicus curiate device was used by the attorney general from time to time, notably in connection with grants of land.[42] The flow of litigation engendered by land grants saw the government appearing to defend past allocations or claimed present holdings. Then, in the 1867 case of *The Gray Jacket*,[43] the Taney Court permitted the appearance of more than one United States agency. In this case, the attorney general had already been heard on behalf of the United States when the Treasury Department sought "leave to be heard" in opposition on behalf of other departments of the government. The Court allowed the Treasury to be heard.

Paralleling the courtesies extended to the United States, state interests also came to ask and receive accommodation. Some state counsel participated as attorneys for private litigants or by admission of state attorneys into proceedings without formal rulings as to status or the extent of participation. In 1864, for example, with the constitutionality of a state statute in issue, the attorney general of California filed a brief.[44] During the 1880s the Court began to grant leave directly to state counsel to appear in an effort to vindicate state rights.[45]

Consequences of the Shift

The change in amicus curiae from an impartial "friend of the court" to a partisan pleader put the attorney general (and the executive branch) in a position to exert powerful influence on the development of national policies. Also, but to a lesser extent, it made it possible for various private groups to influence national policies through what has been described as "judicial lobbying."[46] Thus, the

---
[41] *Id.* at 490.
[42] See, *e.g.,* Dubuque & Pac. R.R. v. Litchfield, 64 U.S. (23 How.) 66, 68 (1859); Platt v. Union Pacific R.R. Co., 99 U.S. (9 Otto) 48 (1879); Mining Co. v. Consolidated Mining Co., 102 U.S. (12 Otto) 167 (1880).
[43] 72 U.S. (5 Wall.) 342 (1866).
[44] Steamship Co. v. Jolliffe, 69 U.S. (2 Wall.) 450, 454 (1864).
[45] See, *e.g.,* Iowa v. McFarland, 110 U.S. 471 (1884); Mining Co. v. Consolidated Mining Co., 102 U.S. (12 Otto) 167 (1880).
[46] See Harper & Etherington, "Lobbyists Before the Court," 101 *U. Pa. L. Rev.* 1172 (1953).

advantages that accrue to bureaucratically sophisticated groups in the political arena became evident in the judicial sphere as well.

Also, the partisan political implications of the change should be noted. Most of the cases in which the attorney general participates as amicus curiae have strong political overtones. Moreover, in many of them the attorney general takes the side of groups deeply involved in partisan political activity, and, of course, he is in a position to decline to appear in the Supreme Court to advocate the cause of a private group if he wishes to do so.

While private groups have used the amicus device extensively, the first consistent use of it for judicial lobbying can be attributed to the Department of Justice. A broader "public interest" approach to government litigation [47] began to emerge under President Theodore Roosevelt. Charles J. Bonaparte's administration as attorney general (1906-09) was a particularly aggressive one in cases involving Negro rights.[48] Bonaparte seems to have been the first to use governmental amicus briefs in an attempt to effect major social changes and implement broad public policies. Specifically, the United States actually was the principal advocate in such private litigation as the *Employer Liability Cases* [49] and *Bailey* v. *Alabama*.[50] And Bonaparte, after retirement from office, personally figured as an important ally of the NAACP in *Buchanan* v. *Warley* [51] which tested the constitutionality of attempts by the city of Louisville, Kentucky, to prevent Negroes from moving into predominantly white neighborhoods. The practice of governmental appearances in significant public causes, where very broad social problems and a generalized public interest are involved, has become standard procedure—as illustrated by such cases as the school segregation, racial convenant, and redistricting litigation.

---

[47] See Easly-Smith, *The Department of Justice* (1904), and Klonoski, *The Influence of Government Counsel on Supreme Court Decisions Involving the Commerce Power* (Ann Arbor: University Microfilms, 1958).

[48] Bonaparte in 27 months conducted 56 cases before the highest tribunal, and personally argued 49 of them. Bonaparte, "Experience of a Cabinet Officer Under Roosevelt," 79 *Century Magazine* 752 (1910).

[49] 207 U.S. 463 (1908).

[50] 211 U.S. 452 (1908); 219 U.S. 219 (1911). Wickersham for the Taft Administration continued aggressively with the case, and the U.S. brief sustains the major part of the legal argument.

[51] 245 U.S. 60 (1917). The case seems to have been a perfect forerunner of subsequent civil rights litigation.

Among the private interest groups that were the first to utilize the opportunities of broader access to the Supreme Court were racial minority groups, securities and insurance interests, railroad interests, and miscellaneous groups under severe attack, notably the liquor interests in the first quarter of this century. Familiarity with the intricacies of the existing system, strong dissatisfaction with it, or a certain amount of desperation all played a role in causing interest groups to seek out and find new channels of influence.

The first example of minority group activity in the Supreme Court appears to have been the participation of the Chinese Charitable and Benevolent Association of New York in immigration cases. Beginning in the 1904 case of *Ah How (alias Louis Ah How)* v. *United States*,[52] Mr. Max J. Kohler was to intervene in such cases, explaining that:

> The peculiar character of these Chinese Exclusion cases, involving arrests or exclusions of Chinese persons, frequently indigent travellers far from their home, and beyond the convenient reach of relatives and friends, as well as of witnesses in their own behalf, has made it desirable for the Chinese persons of the City of New York, and its immediate vicinity, by concerted action and mutual aid, to assist each other . . . and accordingly at or about August 1, 1903, your petitioning corporation did retain Mr. Max Kohler . . . to defend Chinese persons arrested within or prevented from entering the United States. . . .[53]

Moreover, almost from its inception, the NAACP has participated as amicus curiae in litigation. An early case in point is *Guinn* v. *United States*,[54] the famous Grandfather Clause case, where the NAACP argued successfully that it should be allowed to participate because of "the vital importance of these questions to every citizen of the United States, whether white or colored." [55]

Highly regulated groups also were early participants. For example, litigation relating to the regulatory powers of the Interstate Commerce

---

[52] 193 U.S. 65 (1904).
[53] Brief for the Chinese Charitable and Benevolent Association of New York, as Amicus Curiae, p. 2, Ah How v. United States, 193 U.S. 65 (1904).
[54] 238 U.S. 347 (1915).
[55] Brief for NAACP as Amicus Curiae, p. 2, Guinn v. United States, 238 U.S. 347 (1915).

Commission has involved extensive nonparty participation of interest groups (though not necessarily as amicus curiae).[56]

By the mid-1920s each major type of political interest had appeared as amicus curiae before the United States Supreme Court in at least one major case. Since then, the number of cases in which amicus briefs have been filed has grown, as has the total number of such briefs.[57] In fact, by the late 1940s, the Court was beginning to regard them as potential sources of irritation. At the same time they were increasingly significant to the outcome and were even cited by the Court on occasion as justification for the granting of certiorari.[58]

While "discrete and insular minorities" of a financial and commercial nature have found the amicus curiae brief to be a useful and potent instrument, it is the use of the device by civil rights organizations that has drawn widespread public attention. The American Civil Liberties Union has been most active in this—as in other aspects of minority group activity.

Numerous civil rights organizations that developed under ACLU tutelage are now largely independent in orientation and activities. Despite sharp differences in attitudes toward, and methods of, litigation, some lessons of legal strategy have remained a common legacy of the most of them. They also have retained some minimal cohesion in many of the efforts to affect court rulings, as well as in their political activities, although hardly to the extent sometimes portrayed by opponents.[59]

Increased reliance on litigation as a means of vindicating minority rights difficult to obtain through the political process led civil rights organizations, such as the NAACP, the ACLU, and the American

---

[56] See, e.g., ICC v. Chicago, R.I. & Pac. Ry., 218 U.S. 88 (1910). (Seventeen organizations participated in a single amicus curiae brief.)

[57] Harper & Etherington, "Lobbyists Before the Court," 101 *U. Pa. L. Rev.* 1172 (1953).

[58] See Harper & Etherington, "Lobbyists Before the Court," 101 *U. Pa. L. Rev.* 1172 (1953); Wiener, "The Supreme Court's New Rules," 68 *Harv. L. Rev.* 20 (1954); Sonnenfeld, *Participation of Amici Curiae . . . 1949-57*, Working Papers in Research Methodology No. 3 (Mimeo. Michigan State University) (1958), for instances of abuse by amici curiae. See Pennsylvania v. Nelson, 350 U.S. 497 (1956), and Georgia v. Evans, 316 U.S. 159 (1942), for instances where amici curiae were cited as evidence in justification for granting review.

[59] See Krislov, "Book Review," *The New Leader*, April 11, 1960, p. 25.

Jewish Congress, to be among the most active filers of amicus curiae briefs.[60] Labor organizations also have been active, and not only in labor cases.[61] The desegregation decision, the restrictive covenant cases and other important civil rights cases saw a turnout of amicus curiae briefs in such numbers that it focused attention on the question of their use.[62]

Amicus curiae briefs attracted wide notoriety and criticism during the last half of the forties and the early fifties, largely because of this rise in the number of filings. For example, in *Lawson v. United States*,[63] the case involving the Hollywood "unfriendly ten" there were amicus curiae briefs from 40 different organizations. Many groups were both aggressive and open in their efforts to exploit the increased significance of this avenue to interest participation. The National Lawyers Guild, for example, was and is a major filer of amicus curiae briefs. And the Communist *Daily Worker* has made the relation of the amicus brief to standard pressure group tactics even more overt. It has called upon individuals to file "personal" amicus curiae briefs by writing letters directly to the justices of the Supreme Court.[64] Other judicial lobbying tactics include such other devices as picketing (utilized during the trial of Communist party leaders under the Smith Act) and petitions (circulated by the National Committee to Secure Justice in the *Rosenberg* case). Similarly a campaign of telegrams was part of the effort to save the life of Willie McGee, who had been sentenced to death in Mississippi. Mr. Justice Black, who had been generally sympathetic to interest group expression, found this a repugnant development and condemned the "growing practice of sending telegrams to judges in order to have cases decided by pressure." He refused to read them and noted that "counsel in this case has assured me they were not responsible for these telegrams." [65]

The amicus curiae brief as a vehicle for propaganda. A lack of discretion—the ignoring of the traditions and practices of the judicial

---

[60] Sonnenfeld, *Participation of Amici Curiae by Filing Briefs and Presenting Oral Argument in Decisions of the Supreme Court, 1949-57* 11, 16 (Michigan State University Governmental Research Bureau, 1958).

[61] See. e.g., Shelley v. Kraemer, 334 U.S. 1 (1948).

[62] See Wiener, "The Supreme Court's New Rules," 68 *Harv. L. Rev.* 20 (1954).

[63] 176 F. 2d 49 (D.C. Cir. 1949), *cert. denied*, 339 U.S. 934 (1950).

[64] Harper & Etherington, "Lobbyists Before the Court," 101 *U. Pa. L. Rev.* 1172-73 (1953).

[65] Vose, "Litigation as a Form of Pressure Group Activity," 319 *Annals* 29 (September 1958); *New York Times*, March 16, 1951, p. 23, col. 4.

process—has even been demonstrated by a few attorneys. Wiener characterizes a brief in *Girouard* v. *United States* as preoccupied with propaganda and purposely ignoring the decisive issue on which the case turned.[66] Similarly, the American Newspaper Publishers brief in *Craig* v. *Harvey* [67] evoked a strong response from Mr. Justice Jackson indicating that he thought its emphasis on the size and power of the constituent newspapers was neither of legal significance nor an accident but simply intimidation.

The question of the proper relationship of an amicus to the principal party and the principal legal question is a complex one. A simple endorsement of the basic brief of a party adds nothing to the cause except the prestige of the group making the endorsement. This is to invite the charge of group pressure. On the other hand concentrating on purely legal argument has its problems as well. Some amicus curiae briefs have, of course, been of great legal guidance to the Court—Mr. Justice Frankfurter relied greatly upon the Synagogue Council of America brief in the *McCollum* case, for example.[68] This, however, occurs generally when the legal talent arrayed on the side supported by amicus curiae is weak, or when the interest of the amicus curiae is, in fact, very sharply differentiated from that of the principal litigants. But these cases are not the run-of-the-mill ones. In most instances the situation is less stark and the considerations more complex.[69]

Where there is relatively adequate representation of the basic points of view, the amicus curiae, however, may perform a subsidiary role by introducing subtle variations of the basic argument, or emotive and even questionable arguments that might result in a successful verdict but are too risky to be embraced by the principal litigant. Generally, arguments that might anger the justices, doctrines that have not yet been found legally acceptable, and emotive presentations that have little legal standing can best be utilized by the amicus rather than the principals. The NAACP, for example, suggested the overruling of the "separate, but equal" doctrine *(Plessy* v. *Ferguson)*

---

[66] Wiener, "The Supreme Court's New Rules," 68 *Harv. L. Rev.* 20, 80 n.296 (1954).

[67] 331 U.S. 367, 397 (1947).

[68] McCollum v. Board of Education, 333 U.S. 203, 229 n.19 (1948).

[69] See generally Harper & Etherington, "Lobbyists Before the Court," 101 *U. Pa. L. Rev.* 1172 (1953).

as an amicus curiae in *Henderson* v. *United States*.⁷⁰ And sometimes such suggestions bear fruit. For example, the ACLU amicus curiae brief was apparently influential in the overturning of *Wolf* v. *Colorado*.⁷¹

Amicus curiae as the court's advocate. Participation as "friend of the court" need not be at an amicus' own initiative, for a court may request it. It is not unusual for the Department of Justice and representatives of other governmental units to be invited by the Supreme Court to participate.

A federal court may also call upon members of the bar (or more usually the attorney general) to act directly on behalf of the court itself. "After all," Justice Frankfurter observed in *Universal Oil Products Company* v. *Root Refining Co.*,⁷² a "federal court can always call on law officers of the United States to serve as amici." Here, in a sense, the old private relationship of the lawyer to the court is recreated, but the officer becomes an advocate for the court itself. Indeed "friendship" at this point becomes a peculiar sort of advocacy. The amicus becomes the spokesman for court interests in a vital and active sense. This is well borne out in the recent cases involving desegregation. When the Supreme Court delegated the implementation of its desegregation decision to the district courts, it burdened them with an unusual amount of decision and activity.⁷³ Where defiance of court orders has occurred, the district courts have called upon the Department of Justice to provide counsel, amici curiae, to support their orders.

In the integration crisis at Little Rock, Arkansas, and the University of Mississippi, the federal district court, on its own initiative, designated the United States attorney general and the United States attorney as amici—and specifically instructed them to carry out activities on behalf of the court. On September 9, 1957, the district court in Arkansas invited the attorney general and the United States attorney to appear as amici curiae and authorized them "to submit pleadings, evidence, arguments, and briefs and to file a petition

---

⁷⁰ Brief for NAACP as Amicus Curiae, Henderson v. United States, 314 U.S. 625 (1941).

⁷¹ For the role of the amicus curiae and of the principal litigant see the dissenting opinion of Mr. Justice Harlan, Mapp v. Ohio, 367 U.S. 643, 675 n.5 (1961).

⁷² 328 U.S. 575, 581 (1945).

⁷³ See Peltason, *Fifty-Eight Lonely Men* (1961).

for injunctive relief to prevent obstructions to the carrying out of the court's orders." [74]

On appeal to the Court of Appeals for the Eighth Circuit, the Arkansas case was styled *Faubus* v. *United States* (amicus curiae).[75] Among other claims, the attorneys for Governor Faubus argued that the United States had no standing to file such a petition for injunctive relief, and that the court had erred in giving the United States such powers. The Court of Appeals, however, found this to be in accordance with past procedure, that it was "proper for the court to do all that reasonably and lawfully could be done to protect and effectuate its orders and judgments." The District Court had acted properly in asking the law officers of the United States to act on its behalf for it "could not with propriety employ private counsel to do the necessary investigative and legal work. It has, we think, always in the past been customary for the federal district court to call upon the law officers of the United States for aid and advice in comparable situations." [76]

There was no need to go into the legal theory too thoroughly, the Court of Appeals pointed out, inasmuch as the plaintiffs in the Aaron case were still real parties in interest and had joined the government in requesting this injunction. Nonetheless, the Court of Appeals emphatically upheld the authority both of the court and its *amici:*

> In our opinion the status of the attorney general and the United States Attorney was something more than that of mere amici curiae in private litigation. They were acting under the authority and direction of the court to take such action as was necessary to prevent its orders and judgments from being frustrated and to represent the public interest in the due administration of justice.[77]

Similarly, on September 18, 1962, when it became obvious that the State of Mississippi was defying the court orders in *Meredith* v. *Fair*,[78] the United States was designated as amicus curiae by the

---
[74] Aaron v. Cooper, 156 F. Supp. 220 (E.D. Ark. 1957).
[75] 254 F. 2d. 797 (8th Cir. 1958).
[76] *Ibid.* at 805.
[77] *Ibid.*
[78] 7 Race Rel. L. Rep. 748 (1962); see Meredith v. Fair, 199 F. Supp. 754 (S.D. Miss. 1961).

Court of Appeals of the Fifth Circuit. It was authorized to appear before the Court of Appeals and the District Court for the Southern District of Mississippi

> . . . with the right to submit pleadings, evidence, arguments and briefs and to initiate such further proceedings, including proceedings for injunctive relief and proceedings for contempt of court, as may be appropriate in order to maintain and preserve the due administration of justice and the integrity of the judicial processes of the United States.[79]

Two days later the amicus curiae asked for an injunction to prevent enforcement of a bill signed by the governor the same day that would have prevented Meredith from enrolling in the University of Mississippi. The sheriff was also enjoined from proceeding on a perjury charge in connection with a previous enrollment by Meredith.[80] On federal initiative, a temporary restraining order was also issued by the Court of Appeals on September 25, enjoining the State of Mississippi, the governor, and numerous officials from interfering with Meredith's enrollment, as well as enjoining numerous legal steps that were leading toward this end, including the filing of actions in the state courts.[81]

The governor was convicted of contempt after evidence "on behalf of the United States and of the appellant," [82] and the lieutenant governor was found guilty upon presentation only of "evidence on behalf of the United States." [83] In both instances the contempt was of the September 25 order of the Court of Appeals which had been issued upon the application of the amicus curiae.

Later, in December, acting under orders from the court, the federal government, as amicus curiae, moved to have the governor found in criminal contempt because of his continuous criticism of the processes of integration and his consequent failure to comply with the previous contempt order. The Department of Justice contended that its participation in this fashion was proper because of "the sovereign's independent concern for preserving the integrity

---

[79] 7 Race Rel. L. Rep. 740 (1962).
[80] *Ibid.* at 752-53.
[81] *Ibid.* at 756-57.
[82] *Ibid.* at 761.
[83] *Ibid.* at 762.

of its courts and vindicating their authority." However, as pointed out by Mr. Justice Goldberg, joined by Chief Justice Warren and Justice Douglas, "Its ultimate interest—securing compliance with the courts' orders requiring Meredith's admission—was identical with the interest of the private plaintiff, and it was invited by the court to render necessary aid in that direction." [84]

Intervention as a "Party"

In legal parlance a friend of the court is not a "party," although under current practice the line between the attorney general's role as amicus curiae and his role as a party is sometimes difficult to discern.[85] But the rules governing intervention as a formal party ("intervenor") are more precise and exacting than the bench-made criteria for participation as amicus curiae. The desire to circumvent these rules has been a major factor in the expansion of the role of amicus.

Federal Rules of Civil Procedure. Special statutory provisions authorize the attorney general to intervene as a party under certain circumstances, or he may become a party provided he meets the more general tests set forth in the Federal Rules of Civil Procedure. These rules, applicable to private parties as well as the attorney general were promulgated and became effective pursuant to authority enacted by Congress.[86]

In order to intervene as a party—to become an "intervenor" in legal parlance—the applicant must have a real stake in the outcome. The Federal Rules of Civil Procedure provide that anyone has the *right* to intervene in a civil suit and become a party if it appears (1) that he has a real interest relating to the *"property* or *transaction"* involved, (2) that he is so situated that the outcome of the suit may as a practical matter "impair or impede his ability to protect that interest," (3) that there is a fair probability that his interest will not be adequately represented by existing parties, or (4) the right to intervene under the circumstances has been conferred by a special act of Congress.

---

[84] See, for example, United States v. Barnett, 376 U.S. 738 (1964).

[85] See, for example, United States v. Barnett, 376 U.S. 681, 688 (1964).

[86] The Federal Rules of Civil Procedure, applicable in the federal district courts, were prescribed by the Supreme Court under authority delegated by Congress (28 U.S.C.A. 2072).

The federal rules also provide that a court "may" permit a person to intervene as a party where he presents a claim or defense involving a question of law or fact in common with the main action. If a claim or defense in an action is based upon "a statute or executive order administered by a federal or state governmental officer or agency," the court "may" permit such officer or agency to intervene. Under the discretionary ("permissive") provisions of the rules, the court is required to consider whether intervention will unduly delay or prejudice the adjudication of the rights of the original parties." [87]

The Congress has also provided that the attorney general shall have "all of the rights [and liabilities] of a party" in any federal suit in which the constitutionality of an Act of Congress is questioned.[88]

Supreme Court Rules

The present rules of the Supreme Court regard an amicus curiae brief as a brief for "the party supported" by such a brief and refer to oral argument by amicus curiae "on the side of such party." [89]

Government Briefs Favored

The rules require, among other things, that an amicus curiae may file a brief "when accompanied by written consent of all of the parties to the case." When consent of the parties is refused such a brief may not be filed without the Court's permission. But the rules also provide that consent *need not be obtained* when an amicus brief is sponsored by the Department of Justice.

Thus, the Supreme Court permits the Department of Justice—but not private counsel—to file a brief as amicus curiae without obtaining the consent of the parties or leave of the Court. Similarly, the Federal Rules for the U.S. Courts of Appeals, which are prescribed by the Supreme Court, provide that "consent or leave shall not be required when the brief is presented by the United States or an officer or agency thereof. . . ." [90] Moreover, a motion

---

[87] Federal Rules of Civil Procedure, 28 U.S.C.A., Rule 24. See also 28 U.S.C.A. 2348.
[88] 28 U.S.C.A. 2403.
[89] Rules 42 and 44, Rules of the Supreme Court of the United States as revised and adopted June 12, 1967.
[90] Rule 29.

by private counsel for leave to file a brief as amicus curiae must show "facts or questions of law that have not been, or reasons for believing that they will not adequately be, presented by the parties, and their relevancy to the disposition of the case. . . ." [91] But this does not apply to the attorney general. In other words, he may file a brief for one side of a suit between private parties without showing that there is any reason to believe that the side supported will not be adequately represented by private counsel.[92]

Oral Argument by Government as Amicus Curiae Favored

The Supreme Court's rules with regard to oral argument by amicus curiae also favor the government. Special leave of the Court is required for oral argument unless one of the parties releases a part of his time to an amicus curiae. And the rules warn that motions for such leave—where amicus curiae cannot obtain time from a party—"are not favored"—*"unless made on behalf of the United States."* [93]

Growth of the Attorney General's Role As "A Friend of the Court" [94]

As shown in the table below, the department's role as amicus curiae has grown significantly during the 1960s. During the first half of the 12 terms covered by the table, government participation in the Supreme Court as amicus curiae averaged approximately four cases per term.[95] During the subsequent period (under Kennedy, Katzenbach, and Clark) the average was 15.5 cases per term). During the 1967 term of the Supreme Court the attorney general became involved in 41 cases as "a friend of the court." Eighteen of these were argued or decided during the term. In the other 23 cases the government filed briefs or memoranda at the petition or appeal stage.

---

[91] Rule 42.

[92] Compare the Court's former rule that where a party has qualified counsel "the need of assistance [by amicus curiae] cannot be assumed" (N. Securities Co. v. United States, 191 U.S. 555, 1903).

[93] Rule 44.

[94] In most cases the attorney general is represented in court by the solicitor general or others acting under his direction (28 U.S.C.A. 509, 516).

[95] During this period, under Eisenhower, the department was headed by Brownell and Rogers.

Government Participation As Amicus Curiae In U.S. Supreme Court Cases Argued or Decided

Terms of Supreme Court	No. of Cases— Government as Amicus Curiae	Appearances as Amicus Curiae as Percent of all Cases in Which Government Appeared
1955	2	3
1956	2	2
1957	7	7
1958	2	3
1959	6	7
1960	6	7
1961	9	12
1962	19	24
1963	28	34
1964	16	23
1965	11	15
1966	10	13

Source: 1955-65: Annual Report of the Attorney General, 1966; 1966: The Public Information Office, U.S. Department of Justice.

Illustrative Cases In Which the Attorney General Participated As Amicus Curiae

A review of the numerous cases in which the Department of Justice has participated as amicus curiae in recent years is beyond the scope of this study.[96] However, several are cited here to illustrate some of the broad policy implications of this role.

"Civil Disobedience" Cases

In 1966 the Department of Justice appeared as amicus curiae in support of several groups of civil rights demonstrators. Two of the test cases in the Supreme Court involved 44 persons arrested in Mississippi at various times and charged variously with:

> ... assault, interfering with an officer in the performance of his duty, disturbing the peace, creating a disturbance in a public place, inciting to riot, parading without a permit,

---

[96] For a list of such cases during the 1962-67 terms see page 98.

assault and battery by biting a police officer, contributing to the delinquency of a minor, operating a motor vehicle with improper license tags, reckless driving, and profanity and use of vulgar language.[97]

The defendants demanded that their cases be removed from the state courts to the United States District Court for the Northern District of Mississippi and they petitioned the District Court to take jurisdiction and order the cases removed. They argued, among other things, that they were arrested to deter them from exercising their "right to protest" racial segregation and that they would not be given a fair trial in the state court. The Department of Justice interceded as amicus curiae in support of the position of the demonstrators.

The Supreme Court rejected the arguments for removal of such cases to the federal courts holding that federal removal statutes were not applicable. The Court pointed out that—

> . . . no federal law confers an absolute right on private citizens—on civil rights advocates, on Negroes, or on anybody else—to obstruct a public street, to contribute to the delinquency of a minor, to drive an automobile without a license, or to bite a policeman . . . no federal law confers immunity from state prosecution on such charges.

In rejecting the position supported by the Department of Justice, the Court said that "unless the words of this removal statute are to be disregarded and the previous consistent decisions of this Court completely repudiated, the answer must clearly be that no removal is authorized in this case." The Court said that "issues of policy" were involved and that the position taken by the demonstrators and supported by the Department of Justice would require "an extreme change in the removal statute." The Court recalled that such questions had been raised by the Court of Appeals for the Fourth Circuit:

> If the removal jurisdiction is to be expanded and federal courts are to try offenses against state laws . . . what law is to govern, who is to prosecute, under what law is a

---

[97] Greenwood v. Peacock, 384 U.S. 808, 813, note 5. Some of the demonstrators were charged separately with "obstructing the public streets."

convicted defendant to be sentenced and to whose institution is he to be committed . . . ? [98]

These cases were argued in 1966 by Solicitor General (now Supreme Court Justice) Thurgood Marshall. Earlier, in 1964, as Court of Appeals judge, he had favored judicial extension of the removal provisions in similar situations, but had been overruled by his colleagues. Taking the same position before the Supreme Court as solicitor general in the role of amicus curiae, he argued that the position of the demonstrators was in keeping with the "spirit" of the Congress in 1866 when the original statute was passed. He asserted: "Whatever hesitation there may be to return to the spirit of 1866 . . . must yield to the unhappy truth that a century of cautious waiting has not removed the problem." Denying his argument, the Court held that "if changes are to be made in the long-settled interpretation of the provisions of this century-old removal statute, *it is for Congress and not for this Court to make them.*" In fact, the Court pointed out that the Congress had declined to make such changes. The Court reaffirmed its prior holdings that the removal provisions "do not operate to work a wholesale dislocation of the historic relationship between the state and the federal courts in the administration of the criminal law."

Open Housing

The case selected by Ramsey Clark for his debut in the Supreme Court as attorney general was one in which he appeared in the role of amicus curiae. The case grew out of a contest between civil rights groups in St. Louis, Missouri, and the Alfred H. Mayer Company. In this case,[99] Joseph Lee Jones and his wife, Barbara, contended that their application to buy a house was denied because one of them, the husband, is a Negro. The Mayer Company, developer of Paddock Woods in a St. Louis suburb, rejected the Joneses' application and "helped frame a test lawsuit by giving race as the sole basis for rejection.[100] The interracial couple then asked the United States District Court for the Eastern District of Missouri to order the company to sell them a house in Paddock Woods.

---

[98] Baines v. City of Danville, 357 F2d 756, 768-69.
[99] Joseph Lee Jones and Barbara Jo Jones v. Alfred H. Mayer Company, No. 645.
[100] *Washington Evening Star,* April 1, 1968.

The District Court dismissed the complaint holding that this was a wholly private transaction, that the refusal to sell was not "state action" and that there was no law, constitutional or statutory, against such a refusal to sell privately owned property.

Attorney General Clark entered the case as amicus curiae in support of the position of the Joneses. He argued that the Fourteenth Amendment to the Constitution "of is own force" prohibits a racially motivated refusal to sell and that in any event an "equal rights" statute dating back to 1866 should be construed, in effect, as an open housing law.

The Fourteenth Amendment provides that "No *State* shall . . . deny to any person . . . the equal protection of the laws." But the attorney general argued that "there are continuing legal ties between the State and the [Paddock Woods] housing development . . ." and that while "no State flag flies over Paddock Woods," its existence is made possible by the state, and that facilities such as sidewalks, sewers, parks, police and fire protection, etc., are supplied by or on behalf of the state. Also, the argument continues, restrictions on the use of the property are imposed by the developer under authority delegated to the company by the state. In short, the attorney general argued that the Paddock Woods development is a "private town" comparable to a municipal subdivision of the state and that "the total fencing out of Negroes" from a privately owned community of this size amounts to state action prohibited by the equal protection clause of the Fourteenth Amendment.

The attorney general acknowledged that the Court had held that the civil rights statute of 1866, does not reach wholly private discrimination. But he argued that "at all events, it may be appropriate to reconsider . . . [this holding] in light of the prevailing view with respect to congressional power under the Fourteenth Amendment."

In effect, in this case the attorney general was asking the Supreme Court to decree open housing in large developments although at the time the Congress had refused to act on an open housing law. During the period of the attorney general's participation in the Jones case the Congress was actively considering open housing legislation. The President had unsuccessfully sought such legislation in 1966 and 1967; and, in January, 1968, the same month the attorney general's brief in the Jones case was filed, the President had again urged it upon the Congress—but at that time "there was virtually no hope that this would occur." [101] The attorney general argued the Jones case on March 31, 1968. Eleven days later following the death of Martin Luthur King on April 4, an open housing provision was signed into law. Among other things, the new law made it unlawful, after December 31, 1968, for a large developer, like the Mayer Company, to "refuse to sell . . . a dwelling to any person because of race . . ." (P.L. 90-284, Section 804). Thus, the Congress resolved the question involved in the controversy between the Mayer Company and the Joneses while the case was still pending before the Supreme Court. But the Supreme Court refused to dismiss the issue as a moot question. It took the advice of the attorney general and decided that the statute enacted over a hundred years ago required open housing. Indeed, the effect of the Supreme Court's interpretation of the law of 1866 is to invoke a broader open housing policy than the Congress enacted in 1968.

Intervention in Hospital Segregation Cases

"The King's champion has raised his lance against the King." In 1962 a private suit was brought in a federal court against a hospital in North Carolina alleging segregation of patients on the basis of race. The attorney general filed a "pleading in intervention" in which he argued that an act of Congress (the Hill-Burton Hospital Aid Act) "authorized and sanctioned" the "separate-but-equal" policy of the hospital and he urged the court to declare the relevant part of the act "unconstitutional, null and void." The Hill-Burton Act authorizes a federal-state-private hospital construction program financed in part with federal grants. It contains a general provision against discrimination by participating hospitals, but provides that:

> . . . an exception shall be made in cases where separate hospital facilities are provided for separate population groups, if the plan makes equitable provision on the basis of need for facilities and services of like quality for each such group. . . .

---

[101] *Congressional Quarterly,* Weekly Report No. 15, April 12, 1968, p. 791.

While agreeing that this provision was in keeping with the "prevailing constitutional doctrines" at the time of its enactment, the attorney general argued that the Court should hold that the "Constitution does not permit the Congress to use race as a yardstick in determining the recipients of governmental benefits."

The District Court dismissed the complaint and the attorney general's "pleading in intervention" on the ground that the Congress had not authorized the federal courts to decide complaints of discrimination by what is essentially a private hospital. When the case reached the Court of Appeals, it was argued that since the attorney general represents the "United States" and it is his duty to defend—not attack—the laws of the United States. In his brief the attorney general commented as follows:

> The United States fully recognizes that it is exceptional for the federal government to participate in a suit to urge that an act of Congress be declared unconstitutional. Not only do we acknowledge our general obligation to defend Congressional enactments, but we also are keenly aware of the self-imposed judicial inhibition against passing on the validity of an Act of Congress "unless absolutely necessary to a decision of the case." *Burton* v. *United States,* 196 U.S. 283, 295 (1905). However, as we have demonstrated, we believe that the conduct of the defendant hospitals is subject to constitutional limitations principally because of their participation in the Hill-Burton hospital system in North Carolina. . . .

Counsel for the hospital challenged the attorney general's intervention as follows:

> . . . For the first time in the history of his office, the Attorney General of the United States, the King's champion, has raised his lance against the King. He himself concedes that this action is "exceptional" (U.S. Brief, p. 40), but greater candor would make the word "unprecedented"—the defendants were able to find no precedent for his action, and under inquiry in the court below, the Attorney General was able to cite no precedent. It is perhaps fortunate in these "exceptional" circumstances that the shadow of the windmill at which he is tilting does not actually fall across the present case.

In this case the Department of Justice did not act as amicus curiae, but intervened "as a party." As a basis for following this course the department cited a 1937 statute that permits intervention by the attorney general when "the constitutionality of any Act of Congress affecting the public interest is drawn in question . . . for argument on the question of constitutionality." [102] In its report when this statute was proposed in 1937 the Committee on Judiciary of the House of Representatives explained the need for it: "In cases between private litigants in which the constitutionality of an act of Congress is attacked by one of the parties, no representative of the Government may now appear as a matter of right to *defend* the statute." [103] The committee also had pointed out that the attorney general would be able to seek review in the appellate courts, whenever a lower court decision "is *adverse* to the constitutionality of the statute." A review of the history of this statute leaves little doubt about its purpose. For example, when it was under consideration in Congress the chairman of the House Committee on Judiciary, Rep. Sumners, who was in charge of the bill stated:

> . . . I believe that the membership of the House understands that the bill provides that in any case of private litigation in a Federal Court, where the constitutionality of an act of Congress is drawn into question, the Attorney General may intervene to *defend, solely,* the question of constitutionality.[104]

The Court of Appeals held that the pertinent provisions of the Hill-Burton Act were unconstitutional and the Supreme Court declined to review the case.[105] Subsequently, when the Congress revised the Hill-Burton Act, the controversial provision was deleted.

The attorney general's role in this case was anomalous. Here he acted as friend of the legal order itself, but against his own representational posture. In one sense this was most admirable, but in another, it was literally irresponsible.

Like James Thurber, we may wonder whether it is not as bad to lean too far backward as to fall flat on one's face. In the *Cone*

---
[102] 28 U.S.C.A. 2403.
[103] House Report 212, 75th Congress (1937) p. 1. (Emphasis added)
[104] 81 *Congressional Record* 3254, April 7, 1937.
[105] Simkins .v. Moses H. Cone Memorial Hospital, C.A. N.C. 1963, 232 F.2d 959, *cert. denied* 376 U.S. 938.

Hospital case this notion was apparently brought home to at least some Department of Justice lawyers who were forced to re-examine the nature of their ultimate legal responsibility.

SUPREME COURT CASES SINCE 1961 IN WHICH THE GOVERNMENT PARTICIPATED AS AMICUS CURIAE
OCTOBER TERM 1967

Argued or Decided on the Merits

1. Hughes v. Washington, 389 U.S. 290 (Water—ocean-front property).
2. Zschernig v. Miller, 389 U.S. 241 (1923 Treaty with Germany).
3. TMT Trailer Ferry v. Anderson, No. 38 (Bankruptcy-reorganization).
4. Avery v. Midland City, Texas, No. 39 (Constitutional law—apportionment —local government).
5. Nash v. Florida Industrial Comm. 389 U.S. 235 (NLRB—unfair labor practices).
6. Poafpybitty v. Skelly Oil Co., No. 65 (Indian affairs—oil and gas lease).
7. Terry v. Ohio, No. 67 (Criminal—"stop-and-frisk").
8. Alitalia-Lines Aeree Italiane, S.p.A. v. Lisi, No. 70 (Warsaw Convention —limitation of liability).
9. Tcherepnin v. Knight, 389 U.S. 332 (Securities Exchange Act of 1934).
10. Puyallup Tribe, Inc. v. Department of Game of Washington, No. 247 (Indian treaty—immunity from state conservation laws).
11. Kautz v. Department of Game of Washington, No. 319 (Indian treaty— immunity from state conservation laws).
12. Food Employees, Local 590 v. Logan Valley Plaza, No. 478 (Preemption—labor picketing).
13. Fortnightly Corp. v. United Artists Television, Inc., No. 618 (Copyrights—CATV).
14. Jones v. Alfred H. Mayer Co., No. 645 (Segregation—open occupancy).
15. Board of Education v. Allen, No. 660 (First Amendment—parochial schools).
16. Green v. New Kent County School Board, No. 695 (Constitutionality of "Freedom of Choice" school plan).
17. Monroe v. Board of Commissioners of City of Jackson, No. 740 (Constitutionality of "Freedom of Choice" school plan).
18. Raney v. Board of Education, No. 805 (Constitutionality of "Freedom of Choice" school plan).

Briefs or Memoranda Filed at Petition or Appeal Stage

19. Texas v. Colorado, No. 29 (Original Docket).
20. Purolator Products, Inc. v. FTC, No. 7 (Robinson-Patman Act—price discrimination).
21. Rainwater v. Florida, No. 18 (Criminal—Federal wagering tax stamp— self incrimination).
22. Ober v. Nagy, No. 106 (Determination of heirship).

23. K-91, Inc. v. Gershwin Publishing Corp., No. 147 (Price fixing—copyrights).
24. Moses v. Washington, No. 246 (Indian treaties—state regulation).
25. O'Reilly v. California Board of Medical Examiners, No. 378 (Supremacy Clause—state regulation).
26. Assiniboine Tribes v. Nordwick, No. 387 (Indians—title to oil and gas interests).
27. Colorado River Water Conservation District v. Four Counties Water Users Assn., No. 498 (Federal reclamation projects).
28. Berguido v. Eastern Airlines, Inc., No. 528 (Warsaw Convention—limitation of liability).
29. Snohomish County v. Seattle Disposal Co., No. 548 (Indians—municipal corporations).
30. Bianchi v. Griffing, No. 591 (Legislative apportionment—county governing board).
31. Allen v. State Board of Elections, No. 661 (1965 Voting Rights Act).
32. Aschkar & Co. v. Kamen & Co., No. 665 (Brokers and dealers—Securities Act of 1933). (Will be argued on merits in 1968 Term.)
33. Amplex of Maryland, Inc. v. Outboard Marine Corp., No. 668 (Sherman Act).
34. Universal Interpretive Shuttle Corp. v. Washington Metropolitan Area Transit Commission, No. 978 (To be argued on merits in 1968 Term.)
35. Public Utility District No. 1 v. Seattle, No. 1038 (Federal Power Act).
36. Seattle v. Public Utility District No. 1, No. 1039 (Federal Power Act).
37. Fairley v. Patterson, No. 1058 (Voting Rights Act of 1965).
38. Bunton v. Patterson, No. 1059 (Voting Rights Act of 1965).
39. Whitley v. Williams, No. 1174 (Voting Rights Act of 1965).
40. Block v. Compagnie Nationale Air France, No. 1089 (Warsaw Convention).
41. Banks v. Chicago Grain Trimmers Assoc., Inc., No. 597 (Longshoremen's Act).

OCTOBER TERM 1966

1. Canada Packers v. Atchison, Topeka & S. Fe R., 385 U.S. 182 (1966) (Interstate Commerce Commission—rates) (Louis F. Claiborne, with Solicitor General Marshall filed amicus brief).
2. Lassen v. Arizona, 385 U.S. 458 (1967) (New Mexico—Arizona Enabling Act—trust lands) (Assistant Attorney General Edwin L. Weisl, Jr., with Solicitor General Marshall for Petitioner Lassen). PS
3. Vaca v. Sipes, 386 U.S. 171 (1967) (NLRB—collective bargaining contract) (Solicitor General Marshall for Petitioner Vaca). PS
4. Walker v. Birmingham, 388 U.S. 307 (1967) (Mass parading—criminal contempt) (Louis F. Claiborne, with Solicitor General Marshall for Petitioner Walker). PR
5. Sailors v. Kent Board of Education, 387 U.S. 105 (1967) (Reapportionment—state school boards) (Francis X. Beytagh, Jr., with Solicitor General Marshall for Appellant Sailors). PR
6. Moody v. Flowers, 387 U.S. 97 (1967) (Reapportionment—county board of revenue) (Francis X. Beytagh, Jr., with Solicitor General Marshall for Appellant Moody). PS

7. Board of Supervisors v. Bianchi, 387 U.S. 97 (1967) (Reapportionment—county board of supervisors) (Francis X. Beytagh, with Solicitor General Marshall for Appellee Bianchi). PR
8. Maryland Penitentiary v. Hayden, 387 U.S. 294 (1967) (Search and Seizure—habeas corpus) (Ralph S. Spritzer, with Solicitor General Marshall for Petitioner Maryland Penitentiary). PS
9. Reitman v. Mulkey, 387 U.S. 369 (1967) (State antidiscrimination legislation) (Solicitor General Marshall for Respondent Mulkey). PS
10. Dusch v. Davis, 387 U.S. 112 (1967) (Reapportionment—city council) (Francis X. Beytagh, Jr., with Solicitor General Marshall for Appellee Davis). PR

OCTOBER TERM 1965

1. Hanna Min. Co. v. District 2, M.E.B.A., 382 U.S. 181 (1965) (NLRB—State regulation) (Acting Solicitor General Spritzer for Petitioner Mining Company). PS
2. Swift & Co. v. Wickham, 382 U.S. 111 (1965) (Jurisdiction—3-judge court) (Solicitor General Marshall for Appellee Wickham). Dismissed for lack of jurisdiction.
3. Walker Process Equip. v. Food Mach. Chem. Corp., 382 U.S. 172 (1965) (Patent infringement) (Daniel M. Friedman, with Solicitor General Cox for Petitioner Walker Process Equipment). PS
4. Snapp v. Neal, 382 U.S. 397 (1966) (Ad valorem taxes) (Acting Solicitor General Spritzer for Petitioner Snapp). PS
5. California v. Buzard, 382 U.S. 386 (1966) (Soldiers' & Sailors' Civil Relief Act) (Acting Solicitor General Spritzer for Petitioner California). PR
6. Linn v. United Plant Guard Workers, 383 U.S. 53 (1966) (NLRB—jurisdiction) (Solicitor General Marshall for Petitioner Linn). PS
7. Harper v. State Bd. of Elections, 383 U.S. 663 (1966) (Poll-tax) (Solicitor General Marshall for Appellant Harper). PS
8. Evans v. Newton, 283 U.S. 296 (1966) (Racial segregation—right of association) (Louis F. Claiborne, with Solicitor General Marshall for Petitioner Evans). PS
9. Wallis v. Pan American Petroleum Corp., 384 U.S. 63 (1966) (Oil-gas deposits—public domain) (Solicitor General Marshall filed amicus brief) (Not clear from opinion who U.S. supported).
10. Greenwood v. Peacock, Peacock v. Greenwood, 384 U.S. 808 (1966) (Removal of cases from state to federal courts—assault, disturbing the peace) (Louis F. Claiborne, with Solicitor General Marshall for Petitioner Peacock). PR

OCTOBER TERM 1964

1. Calhoon v. Harvey, 379 U.S. 134 (1964) (Landrum-Griffin Act—jurisdiction) (Solicitor General Cox for Petitioner Calhoon). PS
2. American Oil Co. v. Neill, 380 U.S. 451 (1965) (State excise tax) (Frank I. Goodman argued for Appellant Oil Co. and, with Solicitor General Cox, filed an amicus brief for the United States). PS
3. Brulotte v. Thys Co., 379 U.S. 29 (1964) (Patents-royalties) (Solicitor General Cox for Petitioner Brulotte). PS

101

4. All States Freight v. New York, N.H.&H.R. Co., 379 U.S. 343 (1964) (Interstate Commerce Act—rates) (Robert W. Ginnane, with Solicitor General Cox for Appellant All States). PR

5. American Federation of Musicians v. Wittstein, 379 U.S. 171 (1964) (Labor-Management Reporting and Disclosure Act of 1959) (Solicitor General Cox for Petitioner A.F. of M.). PS

6. Brotherhood of Railway and Steamship Clerks v. United Air Lines, 379 U.S. 26 (1964) (Case dismissed on technicality) (Solicitor General Cox for Petitioner Brotherhood). PR

7. Jankovich v. Indiana Toll Road Comm., 379 U.S. 487 (1965) (Federal Airport Act—case dismissed on technicality) (Solicitor General Cox for Petitioner Jankovich). PR

8. Radio and T.V. Local 1264 v. Broadcast Service, 380 U.S. 255 (1965) (NLRB—jurisdiction) (Solicitor General Cox for Petitioner Local 1264). PS

9. Warren Trading Post v. Arizona Tax Com., 380 U.S. 685 (1965) (Taxes—Indiana reservation) (Solicitor General Cox for Appellant Trading Post). PS

10. Corbett v. Stergios, 381 U.S. 124 (1965) (Interpretation of 1954 Treaty of Friendship, Commerce and Navigation) (Solicitor General Cox filed amicus brief) (Brief may have been true "friend-of-court" brief—impossible to tell from record).

11. Meat Cutters Union v. Jewel Tea Co., 381 U.S. 676 (1965) (Sherman Act) (Solicitor General Cox for Petitioner Meat Cutters Union). PS

12. Associated Food Retailers of Chicago v. Jewel Tea, 381 U.S. 761 (1965) (Sherman Act) (Solicitor General Cox for Petitioner Food Retailers). PS

13. Minnesota Mining v. New Jersey Wood F. Co., 381 U.S. 311 (1965) (Clayton Act) (Solicitor General Cox for Respondent New Jersey Wood). PS

14. Harman v. Forssenius, 380 U.S. 528, 1965 (Poll tax statute) (Harold H. Greene, with Solicitor General Cox for Appellee Forssenius). PS

15. Hughes Tool Co. v. Trans World Airlines, 380 U.S. 248 (1965) (Acting Solicitor General Spritzer filed amicus for CAB). Cert. dismissed.

16. Hughes Tool Co. v. Trans World Airlines, 380 U.S. 249 (1965) (Acting Solicitor General Spritzer filed amicus for CAB). Cert. dismissed.

OCTOBER TERM 1963

1. Griffin v. Maryland, 378 U.S. 130 (1964) (Racial Segregation—Criminal trespass) (Ralph S. Spritzer, with Solicitor General Cox for Petitioner Griffin). PS

2. Barr v. Columbia, 378 U.S. 146 (1964) (Sit-in demonstration) (Ralph S. Spritzer, with Solicitor General Cox for Petitioner Barr). PS

3. Bovie v. Columbia, 378 U.S. 347 (1964) (Sit-in demonstration) (Ralph S. Spritzer, with Solicitor General Cox for Petitioner Bovie). PS

4. Bell v. Maryland, 378 U.S. 226 (1964) (Sit-in demonstration) (Ralph S. Spritzer, with Solicitor General Cox for Petitioner Bell). PS

5. Robinson v. Florida, 378 U.S. 153 (1964) (Sit-in demonstration) (Ralph S. Spritzer, with Solicitor General Cox for Petitioner Robinson). PS

6. Retail Clerks v. Schermerhorn, 375 U.S. 96 (1963) (Validity of "agency shop" clause) (Solicitor General Cox for Respondent Schermerhorn). PS
7. Banco Nacional de Cuba v. Sabbatino, 376 U.S. 398 (1964) (International Law—Act of State doctrine) (Deputy Attorney General Nicholas deB. Katzenbach, with Solicitor General Cox for Petitioner Banco Nacional de Cuba). PS
8. WMCA v. Lomenzo, 377 U.S. 633 (1964) (State legislative reapportionment) (Solicitor General Cox for Appellant WMCA). PS
9. Carey v. Westinghouse Electric Corp., 375 U.S. 261 (1964) (NLRA—jurisdictional dispute) (Solicitor General Cox for Petitioner Carey). PS
10. Wesberry v. Sanders, 376 U.S. 1 (1964) (Reapportionment—Congressional districts) (Bruce J. Terris, with Solicitor General Cox for Appellant Wesberry). PS
11. Reynolds v. Sims, Vann v. Baggett, McConnell v. Baggett, 377 U.S. 533 (1964) (State legislative reapportionment) (Solicitor General Cox for both Appellants and Appellees in different cases). PS
12. Maryland Committee v. Tawes, 377 U.S. 656 (1964) (State legislative reapportionment) (Solicitor General Cox for Appellant Maryland Committee). PS
13. Fields v. Fairfield, 375 U.S. 248 (1963) (Criminal contempt) (Assistant Attorney General Marshall, with Solicitor General Cox for Petitioner Fields). PS
14. Yiatchos v. Yiatchos, 376 U.S. 306 (1964) (Community property-federal savings bonds) (Solicitor General Cox for Petitioner Yiatchos). PS
15. Anderson v. Martin, 375 U.S. 399 (1964) (Elections—designation of candidate's race) (Solicitor General Cox for Appellant Anderson). PS
16. Mechling Barge Lines v. United States, Board of Trade of the City of Chicago v. United States, 376 U.S. 375 (1964) (Interstate Commerce Commission rates) (Frank I. Goodman, with Solicitor General Cox for Appellants). PS [A.G. argued contra to ICC]
17. Davis v. Mann, 377 U.S. 678 (1964) (State legislative apportionment) (Solicitor General Cox for Appellee Mann). PS
18. Compo Corp. v. Day-Brite Lighting, 376 U.S. 234 (1964) (Unfair trade practices) (Solicitor General Cox for Petitioner Compco Corp.). PS
19. Sears, Roebuck & Co. v. Stiffel Co., 376 U.S. 225 (1964) (Patent—federal laws) (Solicitor General Cox for Petitioner Sears, Roebuck). PS
20. Roman v. Sincock, 377 U.S. 695 (1964) (State legislative reapportionment) (Solicitor General Cox for Appellee Sincock). PS
21. Humble Pipe Line Co. v. Waggonner, Natural Gas and Oil Corp. v. Waggonner, 376 U.S. 369 (1964) (Solicitor General Cox for Petitioners). PS
22. J. I. Case Co. v. Borak, 377 U.S. 426 (1964) (Securities Exchange Act—proxies) (Philip A. Loomis, Jr., with Solicitor General Cox for Respondent Borak). PS
23. Lucas v. Colorado General Assembly, 377 U.S. 713 (1964) (State legislative reapportionment) (Solicitor General Cox for Appellant Lucas). PS
24. Griffin v. School Bd. of Prince Edward, 377 U.S. 218 (1964) (School desegregation) (Solicitor General Cox for Petitioner Griffin). PS
25. Calhoun v. Latimer, 377 U.S. 263 (1964) (School desegregation) (Assistant Attorney General Marshall, with Solicitor General Cox for Petitioner Calhoun). PS

OCTOBER TERM 1962

1. Avent v. North Carolina, 373 U.S. 375 (1963) (Sit-in Demonstration) (Solicitor General Cox for Petitioner Avent). PS
2. Lombard v. Louisiana, 373 U.S. 267 (1963) (Sit-in Demonstration) (Solicitor General Cox for Petitioner Lombard). PS
3. Gober v. Birmingham, 373 U.S. 374 (1963) (Sit-in Demonstration) (Solicitor General Cox for Petitioner Gober). PS
4. Shuttlesworth v. Birmingham, 373 U.S. 262 (1963) (Violation of criminal trespass statute) (Solicitor General Cox for Petitioner Shuttlesworth). PS
5. Peterson v. Greenville, 373 U.S. 244 (1963) (Sit-in Demonstration) (Solicitor General Cox for Petitioner Peterson). PS
6. Smith v. Evening News Asso., 371 U.S. 195 (1962) (Concurrent jurisdiction of NLRB and courts) (Solicitor General Cox, *by invitation of the Court* for Petitioner Smith). PS
7. Incres S.S. Co. v. Maritime Workers Union, 372 U.S. 24 (1963) Applicability of NLRA to foreign vessels) (Solicitor General Cox for Petitioner Steamship Company). PS
8. Northern Nat. Gas Co. v. State Corp. Com., 372 U.S. 84 (1963) (Jurisdiction of FPC) (Solicitor General Cox for Appellant Gas Company). PS
9. McCulloch v. Marineros de Honduras, 372 U.S. 10 (1963) (Applicability of NLRA to foreign vessels) (Solicitor General Cox for Respondent Union). PS
10. McLeod v. Empresa Hondurena de Vapores, 372 U.S. 10 (1963) (Applicability of NLRA to foreign vessels) (Solicitor General Cox for Respondent Hondurena de Vapores). PS
11. National Maritime Union v. Hondurena de Vapores, 372 U.S. 10 (1963) (Applicability of NLRA to foreign vessels) (Solicitor General Cox for Respondent Hondurena de Vapores). PS
12. New Jersey v. New York, S. & W. R. Co., 372 U.S. 1 (1963) (ICC Jurisdiction) (Solicitor General Cox for Appellant New Jersey). PS
13. Gray v. Sanders, 372 U.S. 368 (1963) (Reapportionment—County unit system) (Attorney General Kennedy for Appellee Sanders). PS
14. Colorado Com. v. Continental Air Lines, 372 U.S. 714 (1963) (Race discrimination) (Solicitor General Cox for Petitioner Anti-Discrimination Commission). PS
15. Green v. Continental Air Lines, 372 U.S. 714 (1963) (Race discrimination) (Solicitor General Cox for Petitioner Green). PS
16. Silver v. New York Stock Exchange, 373 U.S. 341 (1963) (Sherman Act) (Solicitor General Cox for Petitioner Silver). PS
17. Goss v. Board of Education of Knoxville, 373 U.S. 683 (1963) (School desegregation plan) (Assistant Attorney General Marshall for Petitioner Goss). PS
18. Head v. Board of Examiners, 374 U.S. 424 (1963) (Interstate commerce) (Solicitor General Cox for Appelant Permian Basin Radio Corporation). PR
19. Arrow Transp. Co. v. Southern R. Co., 372 U.S. 658 (1963) (Interstate Commerce Commission) (Ralph S. Spritzer, with Solicitor General Cox for Petitioner Transportation Company). PR

PS=Position of Attorney General supported.
PR=Position of Attorney General rejected.

IV.

THE ATTORNEY GENERAL AND CIVIL RIGHTS 1870-1964[1]

By Robert G. Dixon, Jr.

Introduction

THE OFFICE OF THE ATTORNEY GENERAL, like the office of the President, is a collectivity. It is one of the vast jumble of pyramids which, taken together, make up the grand pyramid that is the executive branch. But to those close to the Washington scene, the office reflects the personality of its occupant and sometimes the personal touch of the President. This is especially true regarding the higher reaches of policy formation, such as the maneuvering that led to the Civil Rights Act of 1957, the Civil Rights Act of 1960, the Civil Rights Act of 1964, and the Voting Rights Act of 1965. But at the level of law enforcement, except for civil rights cases and a few large cases (for example, the Eisenhower Administration's

---

[1] This overview essay attempts to pull together from a variety of sources a "story" not commonly known and still developing. To the following former members of the Civil Rights Division, Department of Justice, the author wishes to express appreciation for responding to many requests for information: John Doar, former first assistant and then assistant attorney general; St. John Barrett, former second assistant; Harold H. Greene, former chief, appeals and research; Arthur B. Caldwell, special assistant to the assistant attorney general. Of course, all evaluations and conclusions are those solely of the author.

attack on electrical price fixing and the Kennedy Administration's pursuit of Hoffa and the Teamsters Union), the personal touch recedes. In the steady pounding of repetitive-type voting suits, habeas corpus petitions from federal prisoners, prosecutions for tax evasion, or antitrust violations, impersonality and bureaucracy necessarily take over.

The Department of Justice therefore is both a highly personal, sensitive, policy organ, and an amorphous collectivity. Both aspects are illustrated in the civil rights roles of the attorney general and his department.

Perhaps none of the many roles of the attorney general have placed him more on public view in the past few years than his role in civil rights. However, he has a less publicized internal advisory function as well as an external enforcement function. For a large range of "frontier type" problems, he is the President's top legal officer and law enforcer.

Below the attorney general, although not closely supervised by him until after the Civil War, is a general field staff—the United States attorneys and marshals in the federal court districts across the country. For the better part of a century these men and their assistants were the only important field staff of the federal government, apart from the personnel of the specialized postal and revenue services.

Insofar as there has been much executive action in regard to civil rights, it has been action of the attorney general and his Department of Justice. The effective starting point is the creation of the Civil Rights Section within the Criminal Division of the Department of Justice in 1939. But perhaps the logical starting point is the Civil War era.

When the torch of civil rights passed to the Radical Republican idealists in Congress after the assassination of Lincoln, a series of statutes were enacted designed to secure the equal legal status of the freed Negro—the amendment to the Freedmen's Bureau Act, the Civil Rights Act of 1866, the Enforcement Act of 1870, the Ku Klux Klan Act of 1871, and the Civil Rights Act of 1875. For a time enforcement action by the attorney general and the United States attorneys stationed in federal court districts across the country, was vigorous. But only parts of these early civil rights statutes have survived to the present day. The crucial turning point against vigorous federal action came in 1883. In that year the Supreme Court, in a sequence of litigation known as the *Civil Rights Cases;* held that congressional power under the Fourteenth Amendment did not reach acts of discrimination by private business where there was no state involvement, thus nullifying an 1875 law which was the forerunner of the present public accommodation sections in the 1964 Civil Rights Act. By implication all other civil rights sections of the reconstruction statutes not aimed clearly at governmental action also became ineffective. Somewhat later racial segregation by government itself was permitted when the Court developed the "separate but equal" doctrine to validate racial segregation laws.

Thus, during the period from the 1880s to the 1940s the attorney general was not involved to any great extent in the field of civil rights. But with the creation of the Civil Rights Section in the Criminal Division of the Department of Justice in 1939, and more importantly with the enactment of the Civil Rights Act of 1957, a new era of governmental concern and attorney general activity began.[2]

The Civil Rights Legacy of Reconstruction

The parts of the reconstruction period civil rights statutes that survived the Supreme Court's rulings in the 1880s were few, and they were defective both in meaning and enforcement powers. Prior to these rulings on the issue of constitutionality, there was a period of major civil rights activity by federal district attorneys in the South operating under the aegis of the attorney general. The first to preside over the Department of Justice, newly created in 1870 to bring together the attorney general's scattered legal functions, was Attorney General Akerman. Although himself a Georgian who had worn the Confederate gray, he regarded the Ku Klux Klan as "the darkest blot on Southern character of this age." [3] Under his administration

---

[2] "Civil Rights" as that term is used in referring to the civil rights organization in the Justice Department, and to the various civil rights statutes, does not refer to the area more broadly defined as "civil liberties." These matters, which fall outside the purview of the civil rights unit in the Justice Department, are excluded from the present treatment. They include such matters as the free-speech issues in sedition and subversive activities prosecutions, the post-World War I "Palmer raids," alien registration and deportation, and the loyalty-security programs including the attorney general's guide list of subversive organizations.

[3] Homer Cummings and Carl McFarland, *Federal Justice* 230 (New York: Macmillan, 1937).

and that of his successor the Enforcement Act of 1870 and the Ku Klux Klan Act of 1871 were vigorously, and imaginatively, enforced.

This is not the place to revive the debate over the true meaning of the Fourteenth Amendment. It contains some "shall nots" phrased not generally but against the "states," the two most important being the provision that "no state shall . . . deprive any person of life, liberty and property, without due process of law," and that "no state shall . . . deny to any person within its jurisdiction the equal protection of the laws." It does seem clear that the Department of Justice, despite the narrow focus of the Fourteenth Amendment on action of "states," had no qualms about interpreting both the Fourteenth Amendment and the Reconstruction Era civil rights statutes appended to it as reaching that private conduct which impeded the Negroes' effective integration into the mainstream of American life. The spirit of the times—1870-80—is depicted by former Attorney General Cummings and Professor McFarland in these words:

> Reconstruction had brought upon the Department of Justice tremendous criticism. "The Inflation of the Attorney General," was the title of an article in the *Nation* in the autumn of 1874. "The control of the troops in the Southern States," said the article, "has been transferred to the Attorney General, who moves them on the marshal's report." The Attorney General, it continued, "has become a kind of political bureau, to which competitors for the government of sovereign States carry their petitions and proofs. Southern governors now report to him on the State elections, on the general condition of the State, on its finances and taxation, its criminal justice, and take his advice as to internal legislation. Political parties send in to him statements of their grievances, and ask him for redress against the tyranny or exactions of the local rulers, and he accepts all the power and influence which the position brings him with great equanimity. He snubs the proud, warns the unruly, discourages the wicked, and cheers on the faithful supporters of the Administration." [4]

---

[4] *Id.* at 248.

Limiting Court Decisions

The high pitch of activity was not destined to last. In a series of constitutional tests, the federal powers, meaning in particular the attorney general's powers, were defined and confined. In one case [5] concerning Ku Klux Klan activity, it was held that the right of assembly and the right to bear arms were rights protectible only against governmental action and were not general rights protectible against private action. In a municipal voting case,[6] the federal statute on which the case rested was nullified because it was not specifically confined to distinctions based on race, color, and previous condition of servitude—even though, in fact, the parties in question were Negroes. In the first round of "public accommodation" suits [7] under the 1875 Civil Rights Act, suits concerning racial discrimination in inns, transportation, and places of public amusement, the Fourteenth Amendment was construed to apply only to state action, and not to the action of innkeepers, railroads, or other private persons or organizations.

By 1883, therefore, the early era of active federal protection of Negro equality had passed, leaving Negroes with victories only in regard to discriminatory jury selection and intimidation in voting in federal elections [8]—and even these had little effect beyond the particular cases in which the question was raised. For a time the Department of Justice turned its attention to prosecution of frauds in federal elections where federal power was held to be plenary. But, as reported by Attorney General Homer Cummings and Professor McFarland, "evidence was hard to secure and southern juries were not easily persuaded. The letters of the district attorneys were filled with complaints or apologies and occasional success was hailed as a major achievement." [9]

At the end of this era the "state of the law" was that only in regard to federal elections did the federal government have broad power to proceed against all kinds of interference, racial or otherwise, on the part of all kinds of defendants, private or public. In regard to state and local elections and the racially discriminatory practices in

---

[5] United States v. Cruikshank, 92 U.S. (2 Otto.) 542 (1876).
[6] United States v. Reese, 92 U.S. 214 (1875).
[7] Civil Rights Cases, 109 U.S. 3 (1883).
[8] Strauder v. West Virginia, 100 U.S. 303 (1880); *Ex Parte* Yarborough, 110 U.S. 651 (1884).
[9] Cummings and McFarland, *op. cit.,* p. 247.

general, the federal government could proceed only against public officials and, if the Fifteenth Amendment (Negro voting amendment) was involved, the allegations of racial motivation needed to be specific.

Rediscovery of the Reconstruction Civil Rights Acts—1939-57

The modern era of federal civil rights involvement began in 1939, as indicated above, when Attorney General Frank Murphy established a Civil Rights Section in the Criminal Division of the Justice Department and charged it with the task of enforcing the handful of provisions of the civil rights statutes that had survived from reconstruction times.[10] The modest nature of this beginning is indicated by the 1947 report of the President's Committee on Civil Rights, which referred to "The Civil Rights Section Experiment." [11]

Statutory Defects

The difficulties were twofold. With a few unimportant exceptions, the surviving statutes did not define with care the civil rights protected, but spoke generally of interference with "rights, privileges, or immunities" secured by the Constitution and laws of the United States. This language posed serious problems of interpretation not only in regard to congressional intent, but also in regard to constitutionality. Criminal statutes must be clear enough to give reasonable advance warning of the kind of conduct that should be avoided. Otherwise they fall into the "void for vagueness" category and are unconstitutional on that ground. Narrow judicial construction of those civil rights acts backed by criminal penalties was necessary, therefore, to save their constitutionality. Civil rights statutes of this type did survive, but only at the price of being rather narrowly confined to acts "willfully" done with the purpose of depriving a

---

[10] 18 U.S.C. §§ 241, 242 (1964). § 242 provides: "Whoever, under color of any law, statute, ordinance, regulation, or custom, willfully subjects any inhabitant of any State, Territory or District to the deprivation of any rights, privileges, or immunities secured or protected by the Constitution, or laws of the United States, or to different punishments, pains, or penalties, on account of such inhabitant being alien, or by reason of his color, or race, than are prescribed for the punishment of citizens, shall be fined not more than $1,000 or imprisoned not more than one year, or both." See also 42 U.S.C. Sections 1983, 1985 (1964).

[11] The Report of the President's Committee on Civil Rights, "To Secure These Rights" 114 (Washington: United States Government Printing Office, 1947). Hereinafter cited as *Report*.

person of some definite constitutional right, such as trial by jury. Hence, in the famous case of Georgia Sheriff Screws, it was not enough, under federal law, to show that the person arrested by Screws was so mistreated that he was dead on arrival at the jail.[12] In the terms of the Fourteenth Amendment, the question was whether the prisoner, a Negro, was deprived of "life" without "due process," i.e., a fair trial. Mr. Screws' conviction in a federal court in Georgia was reversed by the Supreme Court in 1945 because the jury had not been instructed with sufficient care on the "willfulness" of Mr. Screws' conduct in relation to such federal constitutional rights as fair trial. (Mr. Screws later was elected to the State Senate in Georgia.)

The "willfulness" test as a way to avoid trouble under the "void for vagueness" principle does not have equal application to those surviving sections of the old civil rights statutes backed only by civil sanctions, such as an award of damages or issuance of an injunction. But the problem of uncertainty of meaning remains. More importantly, however, these old civil sections are not enforceable by the attorney general. They may be invoked only by the aggrieved private party. In the context of race relations, or police or prison brutality against white or Negro prisoners, this meant that civil enforcement of the civil rights acts was left to the poorest and least influential portion of the community, operating sometimes from behind bars and cast in the role of suing the upholders of law and order. As might be expected, civil rights suits by private plaintiffs were rare.

The common pattern of activity during this period of renewed attention to the surviving sections of the Reconstruction Era civil rights statutes was one of federal criminal prosecution by the Department of Justice, focusing primarily on election offenses or on complaints of brutality and mistreatment of prisoners by police or prison officials. The staff remained small, after a decade of activity, consisting of only seven lawyers including the section chief.

However, for investigative purposes the Civil Rights Section could use the Federal Bureau of Investigation, which has continued to be the primary investigating arm for the attorney general in civil rights as in other fields. The volume of activity during the period in

---

[12] Screws v. United States, 325 U.S. 91 (1945).

question is suggested by figures for 1951 indicating that 1,000 complaints were received, of which 370 were of sufficient substance to be investigated. Although slavery as such ended with the Civil War, it is striking to note that 63 of the complaints received in 1951 were for peonage, i.e., a form of debt slavery to bind unwilling and ignorant employees to their employers. In the first few years of the section's existence, peonage complaints formed a substantial proportion of the work load, but then it declined sharply because of the combined factors of federal pressure and increased affluence brought by World War II.

By the late 1940s and early 1950s, the major effort, as measured by the number of Civil Rights Section cases reaching the courts, was in the area of police and prison brutality—where some of the records were sordid indeed.[13] But the department had found that in all cases—North and South—the vague wording of the old statutes made them difficult to enforce.

The Constitution does not list specifically the personal rights that may be protected by the federal government, and federal statutes, at least until the wave of new civil rights legislation beginning in 1957, did not attempt to enumerate them. A more detailed statutory enumeration, to ease the problem of vagueness and to make unnecessary such a strict reliance on the willfulness test, had been suggested by the dissenting justices in *Screws*.

As one commentator phrased the problem, the willfulness test enabled some defense attorneys to persuade the jury that "virtually none but a constitutional lawyer could violate the statute since others would not be capable of possessing the specific intent to deprive the victim of a known constitutional right." [14]

Report of the President's Committee on Civil Rights

The 1947 report of the President's Committee on Civil Rights summarized perceptively both the problems caused by the vague wording of the revived reconstruction era statutes, and the practical difficulty of trying to administer an effective civil rights program.[15]

---

[13] Screws v. United States, 160 F. 2d 746 (5th Cir. 1947); United States v. Jackson, 235 F. 2d 925 (8th Cir. 1956).
[14] Henry Putzel, Jr., "Federal Civil Rights Enforcement: A Current Appraisal," 99 *Pa. L. Rev.* 439, 450 (1951).
[15] Report, *op. cit.*

The committee noted that the Civil Rights Section of the Department of Justice was created on the initiative of Attorney General Frank Murphy by administrative order, rather than by explicit congressional action; that the section had insufficient staff; that it had to work with a miscellaneous collection of old statutes, the most important of which spoke only vaguely of "rights, privileges, or immunities secured or protected by the Constitution or laws governing the United States"; and that prosecution became more difficult when the Supreme Court elaborated the "willfullness" test in *Screws* as a way of saving the constitutionality of these statutes. The committee also felt that in too many instances United States attorneys, who tended to be sensitive to local feelings and the difficulty of getting convictions, were allowed to become the final arbiters in the disposition of civil rights cases. Another problem was the built-in conflict between the FBI's practice of working in close cooperation with local police officials on general federal law enforcement matters and its function of investigating alleged civil rights misconduct by some of these same local police officials.

The President's committee quoted FBI Director J. Edgar Hoover in these terms:

> We are faced, usually, in these investigations, with what I would call an iron curtain, in practically every one of these cases in the communities in which the investigations have to be conducted. Now we are absolutely powerless, as investigators, unless the citizens of a community come forward with information. In other words, our function is to go out and get the evidence. We have to have sources of information, we have got to be able to go to citizens and have them talk freely and frankly to us, so that we may prepare the case for the prosecuting attorney.[16]

Expanding the Government's Role: The "Amicus" Technique—Early Years

Long before the passage of the 1957 Civil Rights Act a succession of attorneys general—on their own initiative and with presidential acquiescence—had moved considerably beyond the range of operations seemingly outlined by the rediscovered reconstruction

---

[16] *Id.* at 124.

legislation. The primary vehicle for the expanded scope was the technique of appearing as amicus curiae ("friend of court") in major civil rights cases brought by private plaintiffs.

As explained at greater length elsewhere in this volume (see chapter III), the amicus curiae procedure, of ancient origin in English law, provides a method by which interested private parties or government officials may request a court's permission to participate in a suit between other parties without becoming a party. The willingness of courts to give permission, and the scope of activity of an amicus curiae, have varied considerably over the years and among different court systems. In the recent history of the federal court system, permission to appear as amicus curiae has been granted rather freely to the Justice Department, and the breadth of participation has made the government in some instances a virtual co-plaintiff. This generalization is especially true in regard to government appearances in the Supreme Court. In this Court all government appearances, either as a party or as amicus, are handled under the supervision of the solicitor general. The solicitor general, a figure who defies structure chart analysis, may be said to be in the Justice Department without being wholly subservient to the attorney general.

The amicus curiae activity of the attorney general has been especially significant in civil rights matters. As already outlined, the attorney general's power under the reconstruction era statutes was limited to bringing hard-to-prove criminal prosecutions for willful violation of undefined "constitutional rights." The expanded "amicus" device has enabled him to go beyond this limited role and to do two additional things.

The Uses of the Amicus Device

First, the attorney general could participate in suits for federal injunctions brought by private parties and strengthen their cases through the addition of federal legal resources. One of the reconstruction era acts provides that private plaintiffs may sue for monetary damages or for an injunction against any person who under color of law causes a "deprivation of any rights, privileges, or immunities secured by the Constitution and laws." [17] Injunction suits have been filed under this statute with increasing frequency by

---

[17] 42 U.S.C. § 1983 (1964).

Negro plaintiffs complaining of discriminatory treatment under the laws or official policy of their state.

Civil suits for injunctive relief, which commonly apply to conduct in the future, are normally more effective than criminal suits to punish *past* misconduct. Injunction suits are also more effective than suits for monetary damages for past misconduct. This is true particularly where broad governmental policies of racial discrimination are involved, as in public education. An injunction does not impose a penalty for past conduct, but it does require change and is enforceable by contempt of court proceedings. Also civil injunction suits are normally easier than criminal prosecutions in the civil rights field for at least two reasons. One reason is that the standard of proof is lower because "willful" disregard of constitutional rights need not be proved. The other is that the problem of vagueness in regard to the meaning of the civil rights acts is eased because an injunction suit only applies the "new" or "clarified" meaning to the future. Thus no defendant can plead surprise and unfairness and say that a new standard is being applied retroactively to past conduct.

Second, the amicus device enables the attorney general to participate in the case-by-case process of clarifying the meaning of the Constitution in such varied areas as racial discrimination in housing through restrictive covenants, in public education, in public accommodations, and in regard to voting rights. Thus the attorney general, through an accretion of experience in a series of such amicus actions, could become a focal point for continuity in civil rights development and acquire a virtual leadership role.

The extent to which this leadership role has been developed and exercised has varied with the personalities of the attorneys general and their Presidents. A rising trend of amicus activity was diminished somewhat in the Eisenhower Administration, at least in the second term when the emphasis was more on legislation than litigation. The fruits of this emphasis were the 1957 and 1960 Civil Rights Acts. Negro militance has also been a factor in inspiring more vigorous governmental activity. Such militance may be the single most important explanation of the dramatic expansion of governmental civil rights activity of all kinds which followed the freedom rides of 1961, the sit-ins of 1962, and now continues in the later sixties.

Some Cases

As early as 1942 the Department of Justice obtained permission to file a brief amicus curiae in the Supreme Court in a peonage case under a Georgia "forced labor" statute designed to aid employers to bind their employees by making wage advances.[18] But the department's first major use of the amicus device in regard to civil rights matters occurred in the Racial Restrictive Housing Covenant cases in 1948.[19] The Justice Department filed a brief and the solicitor general participated in the oral argument in the Supreme Court. It was the first time the government had participated in a civil rights case to which it was not a party and where its sole purpose was the vindication of Fifth and Fourteenth Amendment rights of private persons.[20] (These amendments are the source of the constitutional rights of due process and equal treatment.)

The degree to which the Supreme Court was influenced by the government's amicus activity in this matter cannot be measured. But the Court did decide the cases in favor of the Negro complainants and, in doing so, advanced considerably the concept of the kind of discriminatory activity covered by the Fifth and Fourteenth Amendments. The Negro community, for its part, placed a high rating on the Justice Department's role. One Negro newspaper gave this tribute:

> The profound and eloquent appeal of the Federal government before the Court on behalf of full citizenship for all Americans marked a high point in this historic struggle. President Truman threw the whole weight of the Executive Branch of the Government behind the fight to emancipate us from these restrictions which have so long despoiled our lives and impeded our progress.[21]

The Court's decision in the 1948 restrictive covenant cases forbade court enforcement of private covenants. In these cases there was not only the "hand of the state" present in the form of state court action but there were also three other factors that seemed to

---
[18] Robert K. Carr, *Federal Protection of Civil Rights: Quest for a Sword* 148 (Ithaca, New York: Cornell University Press, 1947).
[19] Shelley v. Kraemer, 334 U.S. 1 (1948).
[20] Putzel, *op. cit.*, at 452.
[21] *Chicago Defender*, May 15, 1948, p. 14, cols. 1, 2, as quoted in Clement E. Vose, *Caucasians Only* 214 (Berkeley: University of California Press, 1959).

justify the result. First, a willing seller and a willing buyer had entered into a sale contract that would lead to Negro occupancy unless the state, through its court system, was allowed to intervene to enforce a prior group contract, i.e., restrictive covenant. Second, restrictive covenants are commonly group contracts covering fairly large blocks of land so that to allow them to flourish with the aid of court enforcement would be tantamount to placing the important public interest-affecting power of zoning in private hands. The third factor was the qualitative one that, on a scale of "equality values," access to adequate housing on a willing seller-willing buyer basis would rank well inside the minimal importance end of the scale.

Because of these additional factors the doctrine of the *Shelley* case cannot be defined simply to mean that private action ceases to be private whenever the hand of the state or any of its organs is also present. In one fashion or another, through licenses, permits, and inspections, the hand of the state is always present.

After this initial major use of the amicus device by the Department of Justice in the civil rights area, a succession of amicus activity followed. It continued on a much expanded basis in the 1960s. The roster of cases up to 1961 in which United States briefs amicus curiae were filed includes most of the well-known civil rights cases of those years.

In the field of school desegregation, the Civil Rights Act of 1964 finally gave the Department of Justice authority to initiate desegregation suits, within certain limitations. But from the late 1940s the department had participated as amicus in every major case both in higher education and elementary education leading up to the epochal school desegregation decision in *Brown* v. *Board of Education* in 1954. In this case the Supreme Court rejected, unanimously, the "separate but equal" concept. In a key passage in his opinion Chief Justice Warren had this to say concerning the meaning of the Fourteenth Amendment as applied to public schools:

> In approaching this problem, we cannot turn the clock back to 1868 when the Amendment was adopted, or even to 1896 when Plessy v. Ferguson [a case announcing the "separate but equal" concept and thus authorizing segregation] was written. We must consider public education in the light of its full development and its present place

in American life throughout the Nation. Only in this way can it be determined if segregation in public schools deprives these plaintiffs of the equal protection of the laws.[22]

Similarly, in the long and still continuing struggle to implement the 1954 mandate for school desegregation the attorney general and his department have continued to play a major role through the use of the amicus device. A summary through mid-1961 showed that the department participated in four cases in Arkansas [23] (including the Little Rock controversy and the dramatic confrontation of Governor Faubus and President Eisenhower), in three cases in Tennessee [24] (including the peregrinations of John Kasper), in seven cases in Louisiana, and one in New York.[25] Of course when these cases advance to the stage of issuing contempt citations for violations of specific court orders—as occurred in Little Rock, Arkansas, and Clinton, Tennessee—the Department of Justice, in its role as prosecutor of the contempt in behalf of the court, assumes a role more akin to that of party than of amicus curiae.

It is interesting to note that, through these numerous amicus actions, the government was more active in the field of public education in the late 1950s *without* statutory authorization than it was in the field of voting rights, where it had received *specific* authorization in the Civil Rights Act of 1957 to initiate voting suits in its own right. It must be noted, however, that voting rights suits were delayed for three years while the constitutionality of the act was being tested. Moreover, prior to the Voting Rights Act of 1965, such suits proceeded through a tedious process of proof.

In addition to its extensive amicus activity in the field of public education, and its similar role in the 1940s concerning restrictive racial covenants on housing, the Justice Department also has used the amicus approach in cases involving racial discrimination in public

---

[22] 347 U.S. 483, 492-93 (1954).
[23] Cooper v. Aaron, 358 U.S. 1 (1958); Faubus v. United States, 254 F. 2d 797 (8th Cir. 1957), *cert. denied,* 358 U.S. 829 (1958); Jackson v. Kuhn, 249 F. 2d 209 (8th Cir. 1958); 254 F. 2d 555 (8th Cir. 1958); Brewer v. Hoxie School Dist., 236 F. 2d 91 (8th Cir. 1956).
[24] Kasper v. Brittain, 245 F. 2d 92 (6th Cir.), *cert. denied,* 355 U.S. 834 (1957); Kasper v. United States, 265 F. 2d 683 (6th Cir. 1959), *cert. denied,* 360 U.S. 932 (1960); Bullock v. United States, 265 F. 2d 683 (6th Cir. 1959), *cert. denied,* 360 U.S. 909 (1960).
[25] Taylor v. Board of Education, 294 F. 2d 36 (2nd Cir.), *cert. denied,* 368 U.S. 940 (1961).

accommodations, transportation facilities, employment practices, the drawing of city boundaries, and other matters.

In regard to transportation and transportation-related facilities there were a series of cases involving railroad cars, terminal restaurants, and waiting rooms. These early amicus actions were augmented in the 1960s, as explained more fully in another section, by some direct actions which the government brought by stretching its powers under commerce clause statutes. This stretching was accepted in the lower federal courts and has neither been approved or rejected by the Supreme Court.[26]

In regard to city boundaries, much attention was attracted by a case in which the Supreme Court finally nullified an attempt to redraw the boundaries of Tuskegee, Alabama, so as to "exclude" from the new and shrunken city most of the Negro residents.[27]

Summary

Thus, the amicus device, far from being a casual thing, has been a major device whereby the executive branch could enlarge its role in civil rights matters. It has enabled governmental participation and perhaps leadership in the development of new or changed constitutional politics in the civil rights field.

The amicus device, itself lacking statutory foundation and hence not clearly based on a broad congressional consensus, was augmented in these early years by those surviving sections of the old reconstruction civil rights statutes which authorized governmental action in the form of criminal suits. But as has already been shown, these statutes authorizing criminal prosecutions under vague standards were of limited utility and were used mainly in regard to police and prison brutality. They were not relevant to racially discriminatory practices in the broad concerns of life, such as housing, education, and employment, and their total absence would not have diminished the utility of the amicus activity in these broader areas.

---

[26] Robert G. Dixon, Jr., "Civil Rights in Transportation and the ICC," 31 *Geo. Wash. L. Rev.* 198 (1962); "Civil Rights in Air Transportation and Government Initiative," 49 *Va. L. Rev.* 205 (1963); "Transportation—Discrimination, Desegregation and Government Initiative," in Donald B. King and Charles W. Quick, editors, *Legal Aspects of the Civil Rights Movement* 103 (Detroit: Wayne State University Press, 1965).

[27] Gomillion v. Lightfoot, 364 U.S. 399 (1960).

Voices of protest were occasionally raised. For example, the counsel for the white property owners in the racial covenant cases criticized the Justice Department for arguing for one side in private litigation between citizens:

> Neither the records in the present cases, nor the decisions of this Court or any State Court, justify the pernicious statements in the government's brief. . . . The government presumably serves all citizens, yet it charges these respondents and others with ignorance, bigotry and prejudice. It is understandable that private litigants may make statements of this kind in their effort earnestly to press their cases, but the government must not only be criticized, but condemned, for such practice.[28]

But Congress, though not specifically endorsing this amicus activity, did nothing to regulate or limit the attorney general's use of the device. Occasionally a major racial case brought by private plaintiffs did go to the Supreme Court, without the addition of the Justice Department as amicus curiae. For example, in the leading case invalidating the white primary in 1944,[29] the attorney general had rejected the suggestions of the Civil Rights Section that an amicus brief be filed in the Supreme Court. But generally speaking, the amicus device was perhaps the dominant vehicle for broad-gauged governmental civil rights action prior to 1960-61.

The current era of Justice Department civil rights activity may be said to date from 1960-61. Although the Civil Rights Act of 1957 is a significant piece of legislation, its substantive provisions authorizing voting suits by the attorney general were not validated by the Supreme Court and unleashed for major action until 1960. In that year the Civil Rights Act of 1960 also was enacted. And beginning in 1961 increased Negro militance broadened from isolated bus boycotts into massive "freedom rides" and "freedom marches," inspiring broader and more immediate governmental activity than had been contemplated before.

In this current era the amicus appearance is no longer the dominant vehicle for governmental action, but the practice has continued

---

[28] Consolidated Reply Brief for the United States as amicus curiae, Hurd v. Hodge, McGhee v. Sipes, Urciolo v. Hodge, 334 U.S. 24 (1948).
[29] Smith v. Allwright, 321 U.S. 649 (1944).

and indeed been greatly expanded. Conjoined with it there has been some use of adventuresome statutory and constitutional interpretation in order to get beyond the amicus appearance—which requires an initial private plaintiff—and find a basis for governmental initiation of suit in areas not specifically covered by statute. But these continued amicus appearances, and attempted shifts from simple amicus activity to intervention or to initiation of suits, are best considered in the context of the general "new look" of the government in regard to civil rights that was sparked by the Civil Rights Act of 1957. To this we now turn.

Civil Rights Act of 1957

The relation of the office of the attorney general to the 1957 Civil Rights Act is doubly interesting. Not only was the attorney general the prime beneficiary of the new powers authorized by the act, but he also was a prime mover in the tangle of political forces that finally—and unexpectedly to many—produced the first civil rights measure in almost a century. Part of the "political story," up to but not including 1957, is told in a monograph by John W. Anderson.

From Justice Department to Congress

As told by Anderson this is the story of a reluctant President—with "enormus personal popularity" that enabled him to be "impervious to any of the usual political issues"—being brought to the font of civil rights by an attorney general who realized that "support in Northern industrial cities was indispensable for winning a presidential election, but support from the South was not."[30] In the closing days of 1955, even before receiving presidential clearance, Attorney General Brownell directed his staff to begin drafting a civil rights bill. At this time Eisenhower was still recovering from his heart attack of September and was not in a position to be approached on a topic for which he was known to have little enthusiasm. When Eisenhower had taken office, Senator Robert A. Taft had warned that passage of new civil rights legislation was a hopeless cause. It was remembered that President Truman's unsuccessful battle for civil rights had not improved his relations with Congress. And the

---

[30] John W. Anderson, *Eisenhower, Brownell and Congress: The Tangled Origins of the Civil Rights Bill of 1956-1957* (Tuscaloosa: University of Alabama Press, 1964).

matter had become particularly delicate for the Eisenhower Administration because, by 1955, it had lost party control of both houses of Congress and thus needed some southern support in order to pass its other legislation.

Nevertheless, Attorney General Brownell pushed the matter and in the absence of the ailing President, was able to get cabinet approval to prepare a bill with the understanding that it would go to Congress over Brownell's name instead of the President's. According to Anderson, Eisenhower ratified the cabinet's decision and mentioned the matter in his State of the Union message in January, 1956, to this extent: "There will soon be recommended to the Congress a program further to advance the efforts of the Government, within the area of Federal responsibility, to accomplish these objectives."

With this acquiescence, vague as it was, the attorney general and Warren Olney III, the assistant attorney general for the Criminal Division (within which the Civil Rights Section still was located), directed the division to draft some remarkably forceful bills. Their prime stress was not on defining new substantive rights. Rather it was on finding legal means to enforce vigorously the growing list of substantive rights emerging from the Supreme Court's processing of private civil rights litigation, such as the desegregation decision of 1954—which was soon to be expanded beyond public education to include all publicly-financed or controlled facilities.

Four bills were produced. Two were relatively noncontroversial: one provided for a Civil Rights Commission as a bipartisan investigating and research body, and the other for an additional assistant attorney general so that the Civil Rights Section could be elevated to division status. A third bill authorized the attorney general to initiate civil suits for injunction to prevent coercion and intimidation in voting. A fourth, more generally phrased and not specifying particular subjects, authorized the attorney general to initiate injunction suits against conspiracies to deprive persons of the equal protection of the laws.

It was the "equal protection of the laws" provision of the Fourteenth Amendment that underlay the racial discrimination cases brought by *private plaintiffs,* as in the housing covenant cases and the desegregation decisions. Therefore, the primary result of this fourth enforcement bill would have been to authorized the attorney general *in his own right* to bring suits to desegregate the public schools.

In statutory terms, the fourth bill authorizing an injunctive power was cast as an amendment to Section 1985 of Title 42 of the United States Code, a section that speaks of equal protection of the laws but not of civil rights generally. An earlier Justice Department draft had contemplated an even broader injunctive power by using the device of amending Section 1983 as well as Section 1985. An injunctive power attached to Section 1983 would have gone beyond racial discrimination and segregation and covered civil rights generally— speech rights, religious rights, fair criminal procedure, et cetera— because that section pertains to "deprivation of any rights, privileges, or immunities secured by the Constitution and laws."

The third and fourth bills were the heart of the package so far as enforcement powers were concerned, but they also, it turned out, went further than the administration was willing to try to go at that time. The White House cleared the first two bills for submission to Congress but not the enforcement bills.

At this point, according to Anderson, Attorney General Brownell pursued a strategy that resulted in all four bills being introduced in Congress in April, 1956, and, as consolidated in committee, being identified as an administration measure. In the communication sent to Congress, Brownell retained the recommendations for congressional action in all four fields, even though only two bills were attached. At an executive session of the House Judiciary Committee the next day, he described the "four matters" mentioned in the communication, without distinguishing the two bills and the two "suggestions." Then, by prearrangment according to Anderson, Congressman Keating requested that Brownell put the two "suggestions" concerning enforcement powers into bill form, and Brownell agreed. In response to a follow-up question from Congressman Celler, Brownell was put in the position of having to say that he spoke for the administration.

Thus, all four bills were "in," and as administration measures. Anderson summarizes the attorney general's unusual role regarding this aspect of what came to be the Civil Rights Act of 1957 in these words:

In his astonishingly bold tactics, Brownell had deliberately jeopardized his own office to get this set of powerful bills introduced; it appeared that he had, as a Cabinet member, overstepped the line that divided initiative from insubordination. The lengths to which he had gone to bring out the bills nearly caused their death at a later state. To get the bills through the White House, or more accurately around it, he had been forced to conceal their import; and none but a few specialists quite understood them until a moment of appalled enlightenment was to burst on the congressional debate fifteen months later. In that moment the country was to be much surprised at the President's refusal to defend legislation that bore his imprimatur.[31]

For his pains Attorney General Brownell got little credit in the press. The press not only missed the nuances and significance of the three-month interplay between the White House and the Department of Justice that finally eventuated in the bills being introduced in this unusual fashion. It even, as Anderson notes, castigated Brownell without foundation for "arranging" to have the bills introduced so late in the session (April, 1956) that there would be time for embarrassing the Democratic party in an election year but not for overcoming the usual Southern filibuster. Anderson described press coverage of the bill and its progress in the remainder of 1956 '—passage in the House, nonaction in the Senate, its role in the 1956 presidential campaign as follows: "The newspaper summaries of the bill itself were inaccurate as often as not, even in the most reputable newspapers." [32]

Congressional Enactment

The next September, the 1956 civil rights bills, along with some additional provisions, finally were enacted into law as separate titles in the Civil Rights Act of 1957. It was the first civil rights act in almost a century.

The "Title III" Issue. There was one major casualty. It was the bill to give the attorney general power to initiate injunction proceedings against official policies or practices of racial discrimination— better known as "Title III" in the consolidated bill. What had

---
[31] *Id.* at 43.
[32] *Id.* at 96.

appeared to some as a seemingly innocuous procedural provision finally was perceived to be a basis for attorney general intiative in civil rights enforcement in the racial discrimination field generally—including suits to speed the desegregation of the public schools.

The basic thrust of the opposition to this proposed power is well characterized in this statement from the *Times-Dispatch* of Richmond, Virginia:

> It would make the Attorney General legal counsel for the plaintiff at the cost of the American taxpayer. In effect, he would be chief counsel for the NAACP.[33]

And the paper added—in a reference to the expanded amicus curiae appearances by the attorney general—"He's almost that now." The response of the Negro community, or of those generally supporting civil rights and the Supreme Court's desegregation decision of 1954, was—"What's wrong with that?" But enactment of such an enforcement power had to await the Civil Rights Act of 1964 which, with certain limitations, authorized the attorney general to bring injunction suits concerning public accommodations and—if he can certify that private litigation is inadequate—concerning public facilities and public schools.

Despite the deletion of "Title III," the 1957 Civil Rights Act did several noteworthy things. It might be said that while the attorney general did much to promote passage of the act, the act also did much for the attorney general.

The Act's Provisions. As finally enacted, the provisions of the Civil Rights Act of 1957 were grouped under five headings. Part I created a bipartisan six-member Commission on Civil Rights with an initial two-year life. (This period was successively extended by later legislation.) The commission was charged with responsibility to (1) "investigate" written allegations of denials of voting rights because of color, race, religion, or national origin; (2) "study" and collect data on legal developments constituting a denial of equal protection of the laws; and (3) "appraise" laws and policies of the federal government concerning equal protection of the laws.

Part II provided simply for an additional assistant attorney general. Part III clarified some court jurisdiction matters and, with Little Rock in mind and at the insistence of Senator Richard B. Russell

---

[33] *Id.* at 55.

of Georgia, repealed 42 U.S.C. Section 1993 respecting the presidential use of troops. The repeal has been deemed to be meaningless, however, because other statutes respecting the use of troops were left standing.[34]

The heart of the 1957 act so far as the attorney general was concerned was Part IV in regard to voting. This part expanded Title 42 U.S.C. Section 1971 to authorize the attorney general to seek injunctions to preserve voting rights. The intent was to make the injunctive power coextensive with two species of congressional authority in regard to voting, namely, Congress' general power under Article I, Sections 2 and 4 of the Constitution to prohibit interference by *public or private* persons in *federal* elections, and its Fifteenth Amendment power to prohibit *public* officials from racially discriminating in *federal or state* elections. Federal authority does not extend to *private* intereference with voting in a *state* election.[35] However, the general practice of combining the administration of elections for federal officials and for state officials into one unified election process make this distinction immaterial. Part V of the act qualifies the attorney general-injunctive process of Part IV. It gives a right to jury trial *de novo* if the criminal contempt punishment exceeds a $300 fine or 45 days imprisonment.

Enforcement Problems Under the 1957 Act

Enforcement of the limited 1957 act, at least at the outset, was a series of frustrations. In one of its first investigations under the 1957 act—a voting investigation in Alabama—the newly created Civil Rights Commission encountered stiff resistance. Gaining access to the voting records required use of subpoenas supported by the contempt power of the federal district court. A "battle of the judges" ensued between United States District Judge Frank M. Johnson and Alabama Circuit Judge (later Governor) George C. Wallace.[36] The United States finally got the records and Judge Wallace narrowly escaped a federal contempt citation.

---

[34] E.g., 10 U.S.C. §333 (1964).

[35] This statement is true as of the 1957 period, and for some years thereafter. However, the opinions of some Supreme Court justices in 1966 suggest a broadened federal power under the Fourteenth and Fifteenth Amendments to reach private as well as public action. See United States v. Guest, 383 U.S. 745 (1966); see also Katzenbach v. Morgan and Cardona v. Power, 384 U.S. 641, 672 (1966).

[36] In re Wallace, 17 F. Supp. 63 (M.D. Ala. 1959); U.S. Com. on Civil Rights, *Rept*, 70-88 (1959).

In the first two voting suits under the act, the Justice Department's Civil Rights Division promptly was met by jurisdictional objections. The first suit was filed in the fall of 1958 against the election registrars of Terrell County, Georgia, on behalf of five Negroes who had been denied registration. In March, 1959, while this suit was pending, the Justice Department suffered dismissal in Alabama in the second suit filed under the 1957 act. Federal District Judge Johnson dismissed this suit on the ground that the two voting registrars named as defendants had resigned, that the Board of Registrars itself was neither a legal person nor a suable entity and that, therefore, there was no suable defendant.[37]

In the following month, April, 1959, the department's pending suit in Terrell County, Georgia, *United States* v. *Raines,* was dismissed on the ground that the voting sections of the 1957 act were unconstitutional. The vice was not intrinsic lack of congressional power in the area of voting but poor drafting, so that the language of the bill, in addition to covering two voting areas within the range of congressional authority, also touched one voting area outside congressional authority.[38]

In addition to these voting investigation and litigation problems, two other matters caused concern. One was the slow pace of desegregation and the spectre of further mob violence against desegregation court orders. It had been made clear in the *Kasper* cases in Clinton, Tennessee, and in the *Hoxie* case in Arkansas that local school boards may be protected by the inherent contempt power of the federal courts from interference with performance of their federal constitutional duties. In each of these cases the Department of Justice had played an important role. In *Hoxie* [39] it had filed a basic brief, as amicus, on the substantive legal questions involved. In *Kasper,*[40] where there was recalcitrance leading to contempt citations, the department had assisted the federal court by serving in the role of prosecutor of the criminal contempt citations. But the federal contempt power, effective as it might be ultimately, was not well adapted to nipping a mob in the bud and so averting a major struggle. For this a power of arrest was needed.

---

[37] United States v. Alabama, 171 F. Supp. 720 (M.D. Ala. 1959).
[38] 172 F. Supp. 552 (M.D. Ga., 1959).
[39] Brewer v. Hoxie School Dist., 238 F. 2d 91 (8th Cir., 1956).
[40] Kasper v. Brittain, 245 F. 2d (6th Cir.), *cert. denied,* 355 U.S. 834 (1957).

Another nonvoting problem was the evil of dynamitings in the South, evidenced by 77 bombings or bombing attempts from 1955 to 1959. The federal government does not, of course, possess general criminal jurisdiction. But the use of the channels of interstate commerce, either for flight from prosecution or for shipment of explosives, could be construed to be a legitimate matter for federal concern.

Civil Rights Act of 1960

Difficulties with enforcing the 1957 act, combined with a recognition of the gaps in that act, resulted in the Civil Rights Act of 1960. Like its predecessor, the 1960 act may be viewed primarily as a Negro voting act, but it also contains several other provisions.

Neither the Eisenhower Administration proposal, nor the measure introduced by Senate Majority Leader Lyndon B. Johnson, gave the attorney general the power to initiate injunction suits for desegregation, a provision that had been dropped from the 1957 bill. Indeed, in the area of education, both bills were moderate, although the administration bill was the stronger. Johnson's bill called only for conciliation. The administration proposal provided that disobedience of a court desegregation order was a crime and authorized federal education for children of military personnel if their public school were closed to avoid integration, along with federal technical and financial assistance to aid local agencies in accomplishing desegregation. But the general tenor of the administration's position, particularly with respect to using court actions to accomplish desegregation, was moderate throughout. For example, Attorney General William P. Rogers told the Senate Constitutional Rights Subcommittee:

> If we start a lot of litigation it might harden resistance so much it would set back the cause. We prefer compliance to come from the people even if it takes a while. In Virginia there has been a tremendous development in the thinking of the people. I think there has been general recognition these last few months (when some schools were closed) that the Supreme Court decision is the law of the land. There has been general recognition that the alternatives are compliance or no public schools. There has been general recognition that abandonment of public schools

would be tragic. As a result there has been search for ways to comply. I think it would not have worked out as well if the Federal Government had moved in there and started lawsuits.[41]

In a similar vein, he told the House Judiciary Subcommittee that "sometimes progress can be made faster without litigation. If you have everyone in a state against you you can't do much law enforcement that isn't pretty disastrous." Senator Douglas' response was that this view "merely puts a premium on tantrums" and that avoidance of federal enforcement would lead to "nullification by neutrality."

Provisions of the Act of 1960

The measure finally enacted as the Civil Rights Act of 1960 did several things. It created the new criminal offenses of willful obstruction by "threats or force" of federal court orders, of flight to avoid prosecution for damaging or destroying property, and of interstate transportation of explosives for the purpose of illegal destruction of property. Although the existence of these provisions —and particularly the power of immediate arrest for obstruction of a federal injunction—may have had a deterrent effect, they have not yet been of much use in actual prosecutions. The two most dramatic instances of interference with court desegregation orders— Governor Wallace's stand at the Alabama schoolhouse door,[42] and Governor Barnett's marshaling of state forces to block admission of James Meredith to the University of Mississippi [43]—were not met with federal criminal prosecutions. Instead, the federal tactics were negotiation, political pressure, counter-force through the use of U.S. marshals, and—when Barnett persisted—the more flexible process of contempt of court citations.[44]

The 1960 act also extended the life of the Civil Rights Commission and authorized free federal education of military dependents whose local schools were closed to avoid integration.

---

[41] *Civil Rights Hearings Before the Subcommittee on Constitutional Rights of the Senate Committee on the Judiciary,* 86th Congress, 1st Session (March 20, 1959).
[42] United States v. Wallace, 222 F. Supp. 485 (M.D. Ala. 1963).
[43] Meredith v. Fair, 298 F. 2d 696 (5th Cir.), *cert. denied,* 371 U.S. 838 (1962).
[44] United States v. Barnett, 376 U.S. 681 (1964).

More importantly, on the crucial subject of voting rights the act made four changes. First, it required the preservation of federal election records for 22 months and the submission of such records on demand to the attorney general.

Second, at the instance of the Department of Justice, it included an important but much overlooked provision on voter registration. The effect of this provision was to make it illegal to apply a more stringent standard to a Negro applicant than to a white applicant, even though the standard applied to the Negro applicant would itself be constitutional if applied equally to all comers. This could be called a parallelism, or a "freezing" principle. Under this principle as construed by the Justice Department, a state which in the past barred Negro registration for whatever reason, and had freely registered whites under standards more lenient than the state was constitutionally entitled to have, could not shift to higher standards unless it appled them equally to persons already registered as well as to new applicants. In other words, the past lenient standards of a state would be "frozen" into place until the state was ready to make a fresh start by requiring re-registration of all voters under new, higher standards, applied equally to pre-existing voters and to new applicants.

In cases brought under this "freezing" principle in 1963 and 1964, the Justice Department won in a federal district court in Louisiana [45] and lost in one in Mississippi.[46] The Louisiana court held that the state could not utilize a new "knowledge of citizenship" test until there had been a general re-registration of all voters under the test or until the court was satisfied that past differential standards for Negro and white applicants had lost their discriminatory effect. The court also said that a "constitutional interpretation" test was too vague to be capable of nondiscriminatory administration and could not be used. On appeal to the United States Supreme Court, the Justice Department prevailed in both cases. Meanwhile, Congress had added a new law by providing in the Civil Rights Act of 1964 that a sixth grade education should constitute a presumption of "literacy."

Third, the 1960 act included a much overemphasized and misunderstood provision for the use of federal voting referees to expedite

---

[45] Louisiana v. United States, 380 U.S. 145 (1965).
[46] United States v. Mississippi, 380 U.S. 128 (1965).

the determination of voter eligibility. The act contemplated that once a judicial finding was made a "pattern or practice" of discrimination in a given area, aggrieved potential Negro voters in that area could thereafter be registered expeditiously by federal registrars. However, the act did not change the traditional understanding that voter qualification and election administration are committed to the states by the federal Constitution—with specified limitations only in regard to race, sex, and equal treatment. Nor did it dispense with the need for detailed factual determination in each instance as to whether a set of voting qualifications, valid on their face, had been fairly and evenly *administered* to applicants possessing varying degrees of literacy and education. Thus, the provision was not a material advance on the authority already available to federal judges under their broad equity powers. By and large, in fact, it failed in its purpose and resulted, ultimately, in the more drastic Voting Rights Act of 1965.

Fourth, in retrospect, perhaps the most important feature of the 1960 act was a new provision expressly authorizing the attorney general to make a state a defendant in a voting suit (thus making it inconsequential whether or not all of the local registrars named as defendants resigned). In 1960, on the basis of this provision, the Supreme Court was able to reverse the dismissal that the attorney general had suffered in the above-mentioned Alabama suit under the 1957 act, and that case proceeded.[47] Also, just prior to the enactment of the 1960 Civil Rights Act the Supreme Court had reversed the federal district court ruling in the above-mentioned Georgia suit under the 1957 act, that the act was unconstitutional.[48]

The attorney general's authority to proceed with injunction suits against deprivation of voting rights was now on a solid legal foundation, whatever practical problems might be encountered. But, as the Civil Rights Commission pointed out, three years had elapsed. With the White Citizens' Council actively purging Negroes from Southern voting rolls during those three years and the federal hand temporarily stayed, the result was *fewer* Negroes registered in some parts of the South in 1960 than in 1956.

Unknown to those who deliberated over the 1960 act or to the politicians in the 1960 presidential campaign, forces were welling

---

[47] United States v. Alabama, 362 U.S. 602 (1960).
[48] United States v. Raines, 362 U.S. 17 (1960).

up that soon would assert themselves in the streets, busses, and bus terminals—in the form of Negro direct action. These developments would involve the energies and imagination of the attorney general and his aides as legal tools were sought—beyond the apparent meaning of existing law—to keep the movement within the legal order without thwarting its goals.

The Dam Breaks—Negro Challenge and Governmental Response

If the "modern" civil rights era dates from the Supreme Court's desegregation decision in *Brown v. Board of Education* in 1954, the recent or "current" era dates from the freedom rides of 1961. It had its beginnings in the dramatic bus burnings in Anniston, Alabama—and in the less dramatic but highly significant refurbishing of the old commerce clause by the attorney general in an attempt to find a "legal" right and avert self-help tactics. Through these events can be traced the rising political pressure that caused the Kennedy Administration to gradually strengthen its new civil rights bill, the bill to which it was committed by the presidential campaign. And the refurbishing and broadening of the commerce clause led ultimately to the use of it rather than the Fourteenth Amendment as a basis for the critical "public accommodations" title of the Civil Rights Act of 1964, that is, the title dealing with private enterprises which hold themselves out to serve private persons generally.

Freedom Rides and the 1961 ICC Bus Regulations

From the freedom rides of 1961 to the passage of the voluminous Civil Rights Act of 1964, and on to Selma and the Voting Rights Act of 1965, the march of events were swift and, in retrospect, closely interconnected. On May 8, 1961, Senator Joseph Clark (D.-Pa.) and Representative Emanuel Celler (D.-N.Y.) introduced in Congress a series of civil rights bills designed to carry out the 1960 platform pledges of the Democratic party. However, there was no presidential message to accompany them. The following day the *New York Times* reported that the White House had disassociated itself from civil rights legislation, Press Secretary Salinger stating that "the President has made it clear that he does not think it is necessary at this time to enact civil rights legislation." [49] And as

---

[49] *New York Times,* May 10, 1961, p. 1, col. 3.

late as July 23, after the freedom riders movement had raged for two months, the *Times* editorialized:

> President Kennedy did not sound like a profile in political courage when a reporter at his latest press conference asked for his "view of the Freedom Riders movement." He seemed more like a man sparring for time. The words he used, "that everyone who travels . . . should be able to move freely in interstate commerce," had no precise meaning.[50]

In the courts, however, the attorney general had been busy working out theories of the government's right to intervene without need for explicit statutory authority, and administrative regulations based on a broad view of commerce concepts were soon to come.

As the disturbances mounted, Negro leaders filed suits and state attorneys general rushed to their respective courts for injunctions to quell the disturbances—but there was considerable difference on who should be subjected to legal restraint. For example, the Alabama attorney general obtained an injunction against unnamed officials of the Congress of Racial Equality,[51] but was himself one of the defendants in the successful suit for an injunction filed by Negro leaders under the old Reconstruction Civil Rights Act.[52]

More importantly, Attorney General Robert Kennedy filed suit against the Klans and state and local officials for causing violence and not protecting persons traveling in interstate commerce. This federal suit posed interesting questions concerning the standing of the Department of Justice to initiate such an action. The department is not authorized to bring civil suits under the old Reconstruction Civil Rights Acts, and the proposal to give it this general power was defeated in the debates on the 1957 Civil Rights Act. Nor does the department have clear authorization from Congress to take the intiative whenever "commerce" is impaired or jeopardized.

The department's solution was to resurrect and invoke the famous Chicago Pullman strike case, In re *Debs*.[53] In that case the

---

[50] *New York Times,* July 23, 1961, p. E8, col. 2.

[51] Alabama *ex rel.* Gallion v. John Doe, as President of the Congress on Racial Equality, *et al.,* 6 *Race Rel. L. Rep.* 528 (Cir. Ct. Montgomery County, Alabama, 1962).

[52] Lewis v. Greyhound Corp., 199 F. Supp, 211 (M.D. Ala. 1961).

[53] 158 U.S. 564 (1895).

Supreme Court had sustained President Cleveland's direction to his attorney general to obtain an injunction against labor activity blocking the flow of commerce, even though there was no supporting statute. The Supreme Court's opinion in the *Debs* case seems to support two propositions: first, that the commerce clause directly imposes a prohibition against obstructions to commerce without need for implementing legislation and, second, that the President in his own right may use force (dictum) or, alternatively, has authority through his agents to seek a federal injunction to enforce this prohibition (holding).

In issuing the requested injunction on behalf of the government in the *Klans* case in 1961, District Judge Johnson relied squarely on the old *Debs* precedent and quoted with approval this salient part of Justice Brewer's opinion:

> While it is not the province of the government to interfere in any mere matter of private controversy between individuals, or to use its great powers to enforce the rights of one against another, yet, whenever the wrongs complained of are such as affect the public at large, and are in respect of matters which by the Constitution are entrusted to the care of the Nation, and concerning which the Nation owes the duty to all the citizens of securing them their common rights, then the mere fact that the government has no pecuniary interest in the controversy is not sufficient to exclude it from the courts, or prevent it from taking measures therein to fully discharge those constitutional duties.
>
> The national government, given by the Constitution power to regulate interstate commerce, has by express statute assumed jurisdiction over such commerce when carried upon railroads. It is charged, therefore, with the duty of keeping those highways of interstate commerce free from obstruction, for it has always been recognized as one of the powers and duties of a government to remove obstructions from the highways under its control.[54]

On this basis Judge Johnson's injunction could reach private citizen defendants, as well as state and local officials, because fed-

---

[54] *Id.* at 568.

eral power under the commerce clause applies to all action, not just to official action. And, regarding the public defendants (state and local officials), Judge Johnson took the extra step of invoking also the equal protection and due process clauses of the Fourteenth Amendment. These clauses only safeguard people against state and local governmental action, and in most instances the officials were doing nothing. Judge Johnson got over that hurdle by resorting to the theory that state *inaction* resulting in failure to protect the travelers was as unlawful as action of an affirmative kind.

More was needed, however, than a court injunction directed to particular, local disturbances with the freedom of interstate travel. The root of the freedom ride dispute was the practice of segregation in terminals, stations, and stopping places used by rail and bus companies, which had continued despite the desegregation of the trains and busses under an Interstate Commerce Commission order in 1955. New legislation from Congress not being forthcoming, the solution was found in the promulgation of further ICC regulations under existing commerce statutes and their nondiscrimination clauses. The freedom rides provided the impetus. And the Supreme Court a year earlier, in an exceedingly broad reading of the commerce clause statutes, had provided the bridge for going beyond the interstate transportation companies and reaching independent, local terminals and stopping places whenever they constituted an "integral part" of the service normally provided for interstate passengers.[55]

New regulations issued by the ICC in September, 1961, prohibited interstate busses from providing or "utilizing" segregated facilities.[56] The rail situation was less critical and was handled concurrently by successful negotiation.

From the perspective of the policy role of the attorney general, the issuance of the new bus regulations has some striking features. Although issued by the ICC under its statutory powers, the initiative came from the Department of Justice. In addition to providing background data from the FBI (including pictures of segregation signs and practices in Southern terminals, and supporting legal arguments), the department's petition to the ICC included the text

---

[55] Boynton v. Virginia, 364 U.S. 454 (1960). See Robert G. Dixon, Jr. "Civil Rights in Transportation and the ICC," 31 *Geo. Wash. L. Rev.* 198 (1962).
[56] 49 C.F.R. Section 180 (a) (1961).

of proposed regulations. And these, in essence, were adopted. The action constitutes a rare example of the executive branch taking the initiative in requesting specific action from an independent regulatory commission possessed of rule-making powers—on a specific policy matter and complete with a blueprint for action.

Expanding the "Amicus" Technique—School Desegregation

School desegregation was decided in principle by the Supreme Court in 1954, and decreed in the "all deliberate speed" enforcement order entered in 1955. As already noted, progress was relatively slow, partly because of the lack of enforcement powers in the attorney general and the consequent need to rely on private suits. The enforcement picture was changed somewhat by the 1964 Civil Rights Act, which authorized the attorney general to intervene under certain conditions as a party in private suits to desegregate public schools.

Even before the enactment of the 1964 act, however, the attorney general, through an expansion of his activity as "amicus curiae," played an increasingly influential role in the desegregation of public education. Indeed, in some situations the attorney general, with court support, seemed to "go in" as an amicus and "come out" as a party. Although a petition to intervene as a party was denied by a lower court in 1961 in the long-standing Prince Edward County, Virginia, suit—where the schools had been closed—the United States remained as amicus and became the dominant force as the suit continued to drag on.[57] (In a segregated hospital case, however, where public moneys were involved, another lower court granted the attorney general's petition to intervene.)[58] Particularly noteworthy were the cases of the attorney general operating nominally as amicus rather than as a party in the New Orleans school crisis in 1961, in the crisis over the enrollment of James Meredith at the University of Mississippi in 1962, and in the Alabama school crisis of 1963.

The New Orleans Crisis

One of the most complete delineations of the breadth of activity

---

[57] Bush v. Orleans Parish School Board, 191 F. Supp. 871 (E.D. La. 1961), *affirmed sub nom.;* Legislature of Louisiana v. United States, 367 U.S. 908 (1961).
[58] Simkins v. Moses H. Cone Memorial Hosp., 323 F. 2d 959 (4th Cir. 1963), *cert. denied,* 376 U.S. 938 (1964).

possible for the Justice Department under an amicus role came relatively early, in the New Orleans litigation in 1960 and 1961. By this date the private litigation to desegregate the New Orleans parish schools was in its ninth year and, as the court put it, "the record is a chronology of delay, evasion, obstruction, defiance and reprisal."[59]

The case was nearly ended when the state legislature passed the "interposition act," purporting to make it a state crime for federal officers to attempt to enforce federal desegregation orders. Against this act of massive defiance, the United States obtained an injunction, which the Supreme Court later affirmed without opinion.

Concurrently, the attorney general, over the objections of the state, was invited by the federal district court to enter as an amicus but also "with the right to submit to the court pleadings, evidence, arguments and briefs, and to initiate such further proceedings as may be appropriate. . . ."[60] Replying to the state's objections concerning the breadth of this activity, the court noted that the merits had been settled and the only matter remaining was enforcement of the court's injunction. The court conceded that normally an "amicus" is permitted only to file an advisory brief, and not to request orders and initiate further proceedings. But the court felt it was faced with a special situation and explained its action as follows:

> The real objection is to the participation of the United States in any guise, whether as party plaintiff, intervenor, or amicus. It is said that the government has no "interest." Of course, it has no proprietary or financial interest to protect. And in view of the recent Civil Rights Acts, perhaps it cannot voice its obvious interest in securing for all citizens the enjoyment of constitutional rights. [The court was here referring to the refusal of Congress to include in the 1957 or 1960 Civil Rights Act a specific authorization to the attorney general to file desegregation suits.] But that does not mean that the Justice Department of the United States can have nothing to do with the administration of justice or that it must remain indifferent when the judgments of federal courts are sought to be subverted by

---

[59] 191 F. Supp. at 873.
[60] *Id.* at 876.

state action. . . . The absence of specific statutory authority is of itself no obstacle. . . .[61]

On this basis, the New Orleans case became, in effect, a U.S.-directed litigation, almost as though Congress had enacted rather than rejected the famous "Title III" of the 1957 civil rights bill. The only limiting factor was that the United States entered the case after the merits had been settled and only the question of a remedy remained. The Supreme Court affirmed, without opinion.

James Meredith and the University of Mississippi

The most publicized of the racial disturbances in the early 1960s was the long-drawn-out battle to enroll James Meredith at the University of Mississippi as a transfer student, and to keep and protect him there until he completed the credits for graduation. Like virtually all education desegregation suits, the suit started as a private law suit brought by Meredith against the university to enforce his constitutional right to nondiscriminatory treatment in public education. As in the New Orleans schools crisis, the hand of the federal government was not present while the "merits" were being settled, i.e., whether Meredith's application for admission to the state university had been processed in racially discriminatory fashion.

On the merits, among the many grounds used by the state to attempt to justify exclusion were the facts that Meredith's admission application had failed to reveal his prior attendance at Wayne State University and, less importantly, that his Air Force records showed him to be aggressive on the racial problem.[62] The federal court brushed aside these points as minor, after-the-fact rationalizations by the university.

The merits of the case were resolved on June 25, 1962, when the federal Court of Appeals for the Fifth Circuit, after months of litigation, entered a mandate that the federal district court issue an injunction ordering the university to admit Meredith. The court saw no valid reason for rejecting Meredith but saw instead "a well-defined pattern of delays and frustrations, part of a Fabian policy of worrying the enemy into defeat while time worked for the defenders."[63] Even the judge who dissented from the mandate said

---
[61] *Id.* at 877-78.
[62] Meredith v. Fair, 305 F. 2d 343, 356-59 (5th Cir. 1962).
[63] *Id.* at 361.

that the university had weakened its case before the court because "on every ground save one [that Meredith would be a "troublemaker" and a "Little Rock" might ensue] the defenses advanced are not deserving of serious consideration by this Court."[64]

At this point, however, the case fell apart again. The mandate was set aside by a single judge of the Court of Appeals, Judge Ben F. Cameron from Meridian, Mississippi. A month later, on July 27, 1962, the Court of Appeals set aside Judge Cameron's stay, recalled the mandate, and itself issued an injunction which was to remain in effect "until such time as there has been full and actual compliance in good faith . . . by the actual admission of [Meredith]. . . ."[65] After more delay involving further attempted stays by Judge Cameron, a vacating of these stays by Supreme Court Justice Black, and entry of a district court injunction on September 13, 1962, it became apparent that Governor Ross Barnett and other officials were determined to block Meredith's registration for the fall semester.

Thereupon, the attorney general applied to the Court of Appeals on September 18 for permission to enter the case, and was granted "expanded amicus" authority in these terms:

> It is ordered that the United States be designated and authorized to appear and participate as *amicus curiae* in all proceedings in this action before this Court and by reason of the mandates and orders of this Court of July 27, 28, 1962, and subsequently thereto, also before the District Court for the Southern District of Mississippi to accord each court the benefit of its views and recommendations, *with the right to submit pleadings, evidence, arguments and briefs and to initiate such further proceedings, including proceedings for injunctive relief* and proceedings for contempt of court, as may be appropriate in order to maintain and preserve the due administration of justice and the integrity of the judicial processes of the United States.[66] (Emphasis added)

In short, the attorney general, though called an "amicus," was made

---

[64] *Ibid.*
[65] Meredith v. Fair, 306 F. 2d 374, 378 (5th Cir. 1962).
[66] United States v. Barnett, 330 F. 2d 369, 370-71 (5th Cir. 1963).

in effect a party to the action for purposes of securing enforcement of the court's prior orders and the actual admission of Meredith to the University of Mississippi. The language of the authorized order paralleled the language used earlier in the New Orleans school crisis.

After a flurry of activity including continued obstructionist tactics by Governor Barnett, an all night riot on the Mississippi campus, further court restraining orders obtained by the United States on its own behalf, Meredith was admitted. And on November 15, 1962, the Court of Appeals appointed the attorney general to prosecute criminal contempt of court proceedings against Governor Barnett and Lieutenant Governor Paul B. Johnson, Jr. In April, 1964, the Supreme Court determined that the governor and lieutenant governor had no constitutional right to a jury trial in such a contempt proceeding.[67] A year later the contempt proceeding still had not been brought to a conclusion in the Court of Appeals.

Alabama Crisis: Governor Wallace and the School House Door

The same pattern—successful private litigation to get a school desegregation order, intervention by Governor Barnett and his assistants to block execution of the court order, and then intervention by the attorney general as "amicus" with the powers of a full party of record for enforcement purposes—was repeated in Alabama in 1963, both at the University of Alabama in June, and at schools in Birmingham, Huntsville, and Tuskegee in September. In both instances the President also federalized the Alabama National Guard to overcome obstructionist tactics by Governor George C. Wallace.

In the course of the legal proceedings the federal district court in July, 1963, determined that

> ... the public interest in the administration of justice and in preserving law and order and in protecting the authority and integrity of the lawfully constituted courts of the United States made it appropriate and necessary that the United States of America be designated to appear and *participate*

---

[67] United States v. Barnett, 376 U.S. 681 (1964).

as a party in all proceedings in this action before this Court. (Emphasis added)[68]

In this proceeding the role of the United States (Justice Department) was thereafter frankly referred to as "plaintiff and amicus curiae."

The United States also played a major role as the Tuskegee situation stretched out for months. The white students withdrew, "private schools" were set up, and in January, 1964, the Tuskegee public high school was closed. In July, 1964, the attorney general sought a statewide desegregation order based on the control exercised by the governor and his State Board of Education over local boards, but the court withheld that relief, conditioned on future non-interference by these defendants with desegregation orders.[69]

In situations like the one at Tuskegee, the Justice Department is not merely a plaintiff for enforcement purposes, but in effect becomes a plaintiff on the merits too, as fresh issues are raised by improper delaying tactics or by good faith proposal of alternative solutions.

The Issue of a Power in the Attorney General to Initiate Suits to Desegregate Public Education

The amicus activity of the attorney general in the 1960s was not confined to school desegregation suits but included a variety of other racial discrimination matters as well. And the Department of Justice, through the solicitor general, continued its practice of filing briefs in the Supreme Court in major public law cases. Perhaps, the best-publicized examples of this are the governor's pro-plaintiff briefs in the series of reapportionment cases and in the sit-in cases.

However, school desegregation continued to be a massive and intractable problem and questions again began to be raised concerning the advisability of shifting the attorney general from an amicus role to a plaintiff role. Such an authorization would give the attorney general a power to initiate and litigate desegregation suits on their merits, rather than to enter, as in the examples given above, as an "expanded amicus" for enforcement purposes after private parties had obtained a preliminary desegregation order. The attorney general

---
[68] Lee v. Macon County Board of Educ., 231 F. Supp. 743, 744-45 (M.D. Ala. 1964).
[69] *Id.* at 756.

would then have powers in regard to school desegregation comparable to the powers he obtained in regard to Negro voting under the 1957 Civil Rights Act.

In effect, such powers now have been conferred by the Civil Rights Act of 1964, as summarized below. While the matter was still under congressional deliberation, however, a dissident viewpoint on conferring such powers was expressed by one legal scholar not unfriendly to the cause of civil rights in general. Professor Alexander M. Bickel, of Yale University Law School, drew a distinction between an attorney general power to initiate school desegregation suits, and thus necessarily take over general responsibility for school desegregation, and an attorney general power to initiate voting suits under the 1957 act (or in public accommodations as then contemplated in another section of the bill that became the 1964 act).[70]

Professor Bickel's view is rooted in his basic premise that there is merit in the system of private litigation of constitutional rights and private requests for judicial declarations of new rights. This system, he argues, ensures that a rule of constitutional law will become effective only when there is wide agreement about it. Seeking to preserve "the delicate balance between authoritarian judicialism and government by consent," he fears the results of conferring broad powers of initiative in the attorney general:

> Not only would that process of private litigation which, as I have said, is in its totality something of a political process of measuring the intensity and strength of interests affected by a judicial rule—not only would this process be circumvented, with the result that judicial power would be potentially enhanced quite out of proportion to which it now is or ought to be. The Attorney General would gain and share with the courts, at his option, powers entirely free of the imprecise safeguards that are implicit in our present reliance on private litigating initiative. It would be the Attorney General, in the exercise of a discretion for whose control no machinery exists or is easily conceived, who would choose to make existing rules of constitutional law

---

[70] Alexander M. Bickel, "The Decade of School Desegregation: Progress and Prospects," 64 *Colum. L. Rev.* 193, 218-23 (1964); John Kaplan, "Segregation Litigation and the Schools Part II: The General Northern Problem," 58 *Nw. U. L. Rev.* 157, 211 (1963).

effective, or explore the possibility of new ones, for he would elect from time to time to concentrate on enforcement in this or that area of constitutional law. This would be quite a revolutionary change.[71]

There were special factors, he thought, justifying attorney general initiative in the voting and public accommodations areas. For example, with respect to voting, the nature of the right to register and the remedy for discriminatory action lack the complexities of de jure and de facto segregation in education and, at the same time, the proof of discrimination requires massive voting records going beyond the resources of the private party. With respect to public education, both the nature of the right and the nature of the remedy are far less clear. De facto school segregation, i.e., school segregation resulting from long-standing residential patterns, is very difficult to deal with. He summarized his concern as follows:

> If the Attorney General is to decide that this or that case will "materially further the public policy of the United States favoring the orderly achievement of desegregation in public education," how is he to make this decision? To put the matter quite concretely, when is school desegregation to start in Clarendon County, South Carolina, or in Athens, Georgia, or in Columbia, South Carolina, or in Jackson, or Oxford, Mississippi, and in which of these places should it start first? And is *de facto* segregation to be attacked, and if so, where? And when? As things now stand, private parties, parents locally, local Negro lawyers, if any, the NAACP and its corresponding counsel, and whatever other leadership is present and effective in the Negro community nationwide somehow make the decision. The lawyer in charge of the suit in Clarendon County, South Carolina, has been deciding year after year not to push it. One of these days he may decide that the time has come. He may not be able to articulate the grounds for that decision, and it may be right or wrong as we view it afterwards. If we substitute the Attorney General as the decision-maker, must we not expect from him some more orderly, rational, and articulate process? For his decision will have been made at the expense of a dozen other places

---

[71] Bickel, *op. cit.*, p. 220.

which pressed their claims on his resources—the resources of government, to which in principle all are equally entitled. It will be said that we do not displace the private decision-makers by empowering the Attorney General to bring suit, and on the face of things that is no doubt true. But in practice, matters will rest almost entirely in the hands of the Attorney General.[72]

He seemed to believe that, in such a situation, the better course would be to utilize the administrative process, operating under legislatively-clarified standards of "constitutional rights" and subject to further judicial review.

Powers of the Attorney General Under the Civil Rights Act of 1964

In the eyes of many observers the passage of the Civil Rights Act of 1964, and breadth of the act, was due in no small part to the rising tide of Negro direct action that was especially strong from 1961 on. Justice Department activity, in the form of voting suits and amicus curiae support of school desegregation and sit-in suits was continuous in this period but the results were not dramatic, given the dimensions of the problem.[73] By midsummer, 1963, the department had counted 841 demonstrations in 196 cities in 35 states and the District of Columbia. Especially dramatic was the march on Washington of August 28, 1963, numbering 200,000 Negroes and whites.

The detailed story of the Kennedy Administration's decision to propose a new civil rights bill, the successive strengthening of various drafts in 1963, congressional consideration in 1963 and 1964, and final enactment in 1964 merits full-dress treatment. However, it lies

---

[72] *Id.* at 221-22.

[73] The number of civil suits filed peaked at 278 in the fiscal year ending June 30, 1961, and then declined as follows: 1962, 252; 1963, 231; 1964, 215. *Annual Report of the Attorney General of the United States* (for the Fiscal Year Ending June 30, 1964) 184.

The President's Executive Order of November, 1962, commanding non-discrimination in federally-assisted housing was a long-awaited honoring of the famous 1960 campaign pledge to take care of housing discrimination with a "stroke of the pen." (Executive Order No. 11063, 27 *Fed. Reg.* 11527, Sec. 101 (1962). But the Order applied only to future federally-assisted housing for which grant arrangements had not been made prior to the Order; and its command of nondiscrimination affected only a fraction of the home financing in which federal agencies play a part. (42 *North Carolina L. Rev.* 106, at 131, 133.)

beyond the scope of this essay. It is sufficient for the purpose here to indicate that the Justice Department played a prominent role in the story because it was the focal point of the new powers being created. In the fall of 1963 there were reports of important conferences aboard the presidential yacht at which crucial agreements were reached between Attorney General Kennedy and key members of the House of Representatives.[74] And in the spring of 1964 the Justice Department maintained a command post on Capitol Hill.

Signed into law by President Johnson on July 2, 1964, the act was the most massive civil rights measure since the reconstruction era. It gave the attorney general extensive powers under the ten basic titles and one procedural title of the Civil Rights Act of 1964. Of the ten basic titles, the only ones under which the attorney general has no direct functions are Title V, which extends the life of the Civil Rights Commission; Title VI, which provides for cutting off federal funds to recipients (primarily state and local governments) who continue to practice discrimination on grounds of race or national origin; Title VIII, which authorizes the Commerce Department to compile federal voting statistics in geographic areas designated by the Civil Rights Commission; and Title X, which establishes a community relations service.

The other titles, and the roles of the attorney general, may be summarized as follows:

Voting. The 1957 and 1960 acts had given the attorney general primary responsibility for Negro voter registration suits. Title I of the 1964 act was designed to eliminate abuses in the administration of literacy tests for voter qualification. It provided that where literacy tests were used, a person who had completed the sixth grade was *presumed* to be sufficiently literate to vote unless proved otherwise. However, it was essentially superseded by the Voting Rights Act of 1965, noted below.

Public Accommodations. Perhaps the best-known part of the act is Title II in regard to public accommodations, which was promptly challenged but upheld under the commerce clause by the Supreme Court in December, 1964.[75] Under this title the attorney general or

---

[74] "Rights Talks Being Held on Potomac," A.P., *The Washington Evening Star,* August 18, 1963.
[75] Heart of Atlanta Motel v. United States, 379 U.S. 241 (1964); Katzenbach v. McClung, 379 U.S. 294 (1964).

aggrieved individuals may bring suit to require certain types of private businesses to provide nondiscriminatory service to all customers. Bona fide private clubs are exempt but the following establishments are covered:

(a) hotels and motels and similar places that provide lodging to transient guests, but excluding owner-occupied buildings renting five rooms or less (the "Mrs. Murphy" or boarding house exclusion);

(b) a restaurant or other place principally selling food for consumption on the premises if it offers to serve interstate travelers, *or* if a substantial portion of the products sold have moved in interstate commerce;

(c) movie houses and other places of entertainment, and gasoline stations, if the films, players, gasoline, etc., have moved in interstate commerce;

(d) any place of business which is located *within* an otherwise covered establishment and generally serves the same customers, e.g., a barber shop or a tavern located within a hotel;

(e) any place of business that houses a covered accommodation and holds itself out as serving its patrons, e.g., a department store with a lunch counter or a gasoline station.

Title II also forbids any denial of access or service on the part of any establishment because of a state or local segregation law. Under Title II a private person may bring suit for any violation, whether isolated or part of a regular practice. The attorney general may sue only in the latter instance, but the court may allow his intervention in any private suit.

Public Facilities. Title III authorizes the attorney general, upon receipt of a signed complaint, to sue to desegregate public facilities (other than schools which are covered by Title IV). The attorney general must be able to certify that the complainant is unable to institute legal proceedings in his own behalf because of inability to bear the expenses or to obtain effective legal representation, or because of possible danger to his personal safety, employment, or economic standing. Such facilities as parks and libraries are covered by this title.

School Desegregation. Title IV covers school desegregation, but it specifically excludes efforts by the attorney general to overcome "de facto" segregation, i.e., assignment of children to schools to overcome racial imbalance. With this limitation, the attorney general was given power to file school desegregation suits upon receipt of a signed complaint, and after certifying that the complainant is unable to maintain appropriate legal proceedings. In the area of intentional school segregation, governmentally-created and maintained, the attorney general has broad power to direct litigation, scrutinize compliance plans, and creatively suggest remedies.

As a result of the above limitation, the more dramatic and controversial efforts to correct school desegregation since 1964 have not been centered on the attorney general's powers under Title IV. Attention has focused rather on the "guidelines" for desegregation set up by the Department of Health, Education, and Welfare under Title VI of the 1964 act relative to cutting off funds for segregated activities. Whether these HEW guidelines could reach "de facto" segregation in the South under constitutional theories transcending the 1964 act —which contained some limiting congressional language that the court watered down—was answered in the affirmative in a lower court dictum in 1966.[76] The lower court's theory was that a past Southern official system of segregation had left a residual pattern of de facto (unofficial) segregation which the local schools had a constitutional duty to correct.

Discrimination in Employment. The lengthy equal employment opportunity part of the act, Title VII, which was not made effective until July, 1965, confers most of its powers on an Equal Employment Opportunity Commission. The commission's principal function is to investigate charges of unfair employment practices in industries affecting commerce and to try to eliminate such practices by conciliation and persuasion. If it fails, the aggrieved individual—*and not the commission*—may then file suit. *However,* the attorney general in his own right may file suit against a "pattern or practice" of employment discrimination by any person. This short, succinct provi-

---

[76] United States v. Jefferson County Board of Educ., 372 F. 2d 836 (5th Cir., 1966), 380 F. 2d 385 (5th Cir., 1967), *cert. denied sub nom.,* East Baton Rouge Parish School Bd. v. Davis, 389 U.S. 840 (1967). The attorney general's role regarding these HEW guidelines is more supportive than direct. See "Comment: Title VI of the 1964 Civil Rights Act," 36 *Geo. Wash. L. Rev.* — (1968) (in press).

sion seems to authorize, if desired, a short-circuiting of the entire, complex and involuted commission operation described in the remainder of the title. The attorney general also may seek court permission to intervene in an enforcement suit brought by an aggrieved individual after failure of conciliation.

The Power to Enforce "Equal Protection" Generally. A "sleeper" in the act, and potentially a quite important provision, is tucked away in a few lines of Title IX. In effect, this section comes close to enacting the old much-mooted "Title III" of the original civil rights bill of 1957, which was designed to give to the attorney general a general power to enforce the nondiscrimination principle of the Fourteenth Amendment. It reads, in its entirety, as follows:

> Sec. 902. Whenever an action has been commenced in any court of the United States seeking relief from the denial of equal protection of the laws under the fourteenth amendment to the Constitution on account of race, color, religion, or national origin, the attorney general for or in the name of the United States may intervene in such action upon timely application if the Attorney General certifies that the case is of general public importance. In such action the United States shall be entitled to the same relief as if it had instituted the action.

Because this section limits attorney general action to suits already filed by aggrieved parties, it falls short of giving the attorney general the kind of creative responsibility to investigate and police the area that he possesses in regard to voting. But it could easily develop that private suits would be filed with great frequency—and over a wide range of borderline, or conventional but difficult-to-enforce, "equal protection" situations (including de facto segregation). Then the attorney general easily could assume the role of creative tactician under a constitutional clause which, like the due process clause and unlike the voting clauses, denotes a developmental principle rather than a settled norm of conduct.

At present the primary checks on development of Justice Department initiative and discretion in that direction—under this broad new clause of Title IX—are the preoccupation of possible private plaintiffs with more pinpointed objectives and congressional limitations on the staff and resources of the department's Civil Rights Division.

The Constitutional Theory of the 1964 Act's Provisions on Public Accommodation

A word needs to be said about the two landmark decisions that upheld the constitutionality of Title II of the 1964 act, the public accommodations section. In a suit concerning motel segregation, *Heart of Atlanta Motel, Inc. v. United States*,[77] the court's primary focus was on a "right of travel" derived from the congressional power to regulate interstate commerce. Segregated facilities were deemed to have a direct and depressing effect on the volume and character of actual and potential interstate travel by Negroes.

The more dramatic case, *Katzenbach v. McClung*,[78] concerned segregation in a small restaurant 11 blocks from an interstate highway that had not been shown to serve interstate customers. The act covers enterprises whose food in significant degree comes from interstate commerce and, on this basis, Ollie's Barbecue was desegregated. More significantly, the court offered the following additional rationale, beyond the "bare bones" argument that the food served in the restaurant had moved in interstate commerce: It pointed to an interconnection between adequate restaurant facilities and such factors as ease of employee mobility, access to jobs, and even employer plant location. It noted testimony "that discrimination deterred professional, as well as skilled, people from moving into areas where such practices occurred and thereby caused industry to be reluctant to establish there." [79]

On this basis, which reads the interstate commerce clause as creating a general power concerning the welfare, tempo, and quality of the national economy, a showing that Ollie's served interstate food would be unnecessary. It would suffice to declare that any segregation in any facility relevant to employer site selection and to personal mobility of employees is detrimental to the national economy and hence subject to congressional regulation.

---

[77] 379 U.S. 241 (1964).
[78] 379 U.S. 294 (1964).
[79] *Supra.*

Note on the Voting Rights Act of 1965 [80]

The Voting Rights Act of 1965 reversed conventional learning concerning the constitutional allocation to the states of power to fix voting qualifications. And it was upheld in a 1966 Supreme Court opinion which created a new kind of national power—a "remedial" power to occupy temporarily a traditional state government field if deemed necessary for expeditious redress of a violation of constitutional rights.[81]

As Chief Justice Warren noted, the act sets up "a complex scheme of stringent remedies aimed at areas where voting discrimination has been most flagrant," [82] and makes the attorney general the central figure in implementing the act. First, the act suspends all voting "tests and devices" such as literacy tests for five years in those states and counties where a "test or device" was in use in 1964 and less than 50 percent of voting-age residents voted or were registered. The attorney general determines whether a "test or device" was in effect, the Director of the Census determines the percentage and both findings are non-reviewable. Second, in areas found to be covered by the above formula, new regulations may not be put into effect without the approval of the attorney general or a declaratory judgment certifying that the regulations are of a nondiscriminatory character. Third, the attorney general is authorized to appoint federal examiners to determine voter eligibility and certify names to local registrars if needed to effectuate the purpose of the act.

The attorney general, in short, is the key figure not only in the "trigger" mechanism and in the appointment and direction of federal examiners, but also in the subsequent "bail out" procedure to restore conventional state power. In operation the act has affected, almost exclusively, certain Southern states and counties.

Saying that Congress had exercised its authority under the Fifteenth Amendment in an "inventive manner," the court sustained this tem-

---

[80] This manuscript was completed in 1964 as an essay on the civil rights roles of the attorney general from the Civil War to the Civil Rights Act of 1964. The Voting Rights Act of 1965 is a major subsequent act which cannot be ignored. The Civil Rights Act of 1968, enacted while this chapter was in galley, cannot be included but should be consulted. It creates additional powers for the attorney general regarding interference with civil rights, riots, housing discrimination, and civil disorders.
[82] South Carolina v. Katzenbach, 383 U.S. 301, 315 (1966).
[81] Archibald Cox, "Foreword: Constitutional Adjudication and the Promotion of Human Rights," 80 *Harv. L. Rev.* 91 (1966).

porary federal displacement of state power over voting qualifications as an appropriate remedy for past discrimination against potential Negro voters. It said:

> Underlying the [Congressional] response was the feeling that States and political subdivisions which had been allowing white illiterates to vote for years could not sincerely complain about "dillution" of their electorates through the registration of Negro illiterates. Congress knew that continuance of the tests and devices in use at the present time, no matter how fairly administered in the future, would freeze the effect of past discrimination in favor of unqualified white registrants. Congress permissively rejected the alternative of requiring a complete re-registration of all voters, believing that this would be too harsh on many whites who had enjoyed the franchise for their entire adult lives.[83]

Conclusion

Within the governmental framework concerned with civil rights the attorney general and his Department of Justice—specifically in recent years the Civil Rights Division—have been dominant, if not all-important. Almost a century ago, when the Department of Justice was administering the Reconstruction Era civil rights legislation, the *Nation* titled an article: "The Inflation of the Attorney General." There has been a somewhat similar "inflation" of the attorney general's powers and roles in our own time. The often narrow and vague statutory foundation for his roles has at times been broadened by creative approaches toward "standing," amicus curiae practice, and intervention.

Since 1964 we have turned to detailed legislative solutions, and broadly redefined the federal government's civil rights posture, through such enactments as the Civil Rights Acts of 1964 and 1968, the Voting Rights Act of 1965, the Elementary and Secondary Education Act of 1965, legislation creating the Office of Economic Opportunity, and other acts. Under much of this legislation the attorney general, as well as other agencies, acquires various new roles. Under this broadened involvement of federal agencies in civil rights a new role for the attorney general may be—perhaps should

---

[83] *Id.* at 334.

be—to maintain a concern for orderly progression in legal standards, for coordination of the regulatory and expediture approaches toward equal opportunity, and for safeguarding against the more subtle forms of discrimination.

The present status of the attorney general in civil rights combines the old with the new. There is now more explicit statutory language. But he continues his creative role in many respects. Long neglected in studies of American governmental institutions, the modern Office of Attorney General, particularly in its varied civil rights roles, merits first rank attention.

SELECTED BIBLIOGRAPHY

Anderson, John W., *Eisenhower, Brownell and Congress: The Tangled Origins of the Civil Rights Bill of 1956-1957* (Tuscaloosa: University of Alabama Press, 1964).

Berman, Daniel L., *A Bill Becomes a Law: Congress Enacts Civil Rights Legislation* (New York: Macmillan, 1966).

Caldwell, Arthur B. and Brodie, Sydney, "Enforcement of the Criminal Civil Rights Statute, 18 U.S.C. Section 242, In Prison Brutality Cases," 52 *Geo. L. J.* 706 (1964).

Carr, Robert K., *Federal Protection of Civil Rights: Quest for a Sword* (Ithaca, New York: Cornell University Press, 1947).

Chafee, Zechariah, Jr., "Safeguarding Fundamental Human Rights: The Tasks of States and Nation," 27 *Geo. Wash. L. Rev.* 519 (1959).

Comment, "Theories of Federalism and Civil Rights," 75 *Yale L. J.* 1007 (1966).

Cummings, Homer and McFarland, Carl, *Federal Justice* (New York: Macmillan, 1937).

Dixon, Robert G., Jr., "Civil Rights in Transportation and the ICC," 31 *Geo. Wash. L. Rev.* 198 (1962); "Civil Rights in Air Transportation and Government Initiative," 49 *Va. L. Rev.* 205 (1963).

Emerson, Thomas I., Haber, David, and Dorsen, Norman, *Political and Civil Rights in the United States,* Vol. II, Chs. 13, 17 (Boston: Little, Brown, 1967).

Huston, Luther A., *The Department of Justice* (New York: Frederick A. Praeger, 1967).

King, Donald B. and Quick, Charles W., *Legal Aspects of the Civil Rights Movement* (Detroit: Wayne State University Press, 1965).

Konvitz, Milton R. and Leskes, Theodore, *A Century of Civil Rights* (New York: Columbia University Press, 1961).

Langluttig, Albert, *The Department of Justice of the United States* (Baltimore: Johns Hopkins University Press, 1927).

Putzel, Henry, Jr., "Federal Civil Rights Enforcement: A Current Appraisal," 99 *U. Pa. L. Rev.* 439 (1951).

Race Relations Law Reporter.

Randall, James G., *Constitutional Problems Under Lincoln* (Urbana: University of Illinois Press, 1951).

Report of the President's Committee on Civil Rights, "To Secure These Rights" (Washington: United States Government Printing Office, 1947).

Reports of the United States Commission on Civil Rights: 1959, 1961, 1963, 1965, 1967 (Washington: United States Government Printing Office).

Shapiro, Harry H., "Limitations in Prosecuting Civil Rights Violations," 46 *Cornell L. Q.* 532 (1961).

Swisher, Carl B., *Selected Papers of Homer Cummings, Attorney General of the United States, 1933-1939* (New York: C. Scribner's Sons, 1939).

OTHER AEI PUBLICATIONS

BOOKS

HOW BIG SHOULD GOVERNMENT BE? (First in series of 1967-68 Rational Debates), *Paul H. Douglas* and *J. Enoch Powell,* 1968—$4.50.

EDUCATIONAL TV: WHO SHOULD PAY? (Second in series of 1967-68 Rational Debates), *R. H. Coase* and *Edward W. Barrett,* 1968—$4.50.

FISCAL POLICY AND BUSINESS CAPITAL FORMATION (Symposium proceedings, 1967—$7.00, hard cover; $3.00, paperback)

Papers:

Business Capital Spending and Investment Decisions, *Robert C. Tyson*

Tax Policy and Business Investment, *Dan Throop Smith*

Review of Our Experience in Administering Fiscal Policy, *Paul W. McCracken*

Economic Forecasting as a Basis for Fiscal Policy Decisions, *Solomon Fabricant*

Objectives of Fiscal and Budget Policies, *C. Lowell Harriss*

The Blend of Fiscal and Monetary Policies for the Future, *Richard A. Musgrave*

CONGRESS AND THE PRESIDENCY: THEIR ROLE IN MODERN TIMES (First in series of 1966-67 Rational Debates), *Arthur M. Schlesinger, Jr.,* and *Alfred de Grazia,* 1967—$4.50

LAW, ORDER AND CIVIL DISOBEDIENCE (Second in series of 1966-67 Rational Debates), *Charles E. Whittaker* and *William Sloane Coffin, Jr.,* 1967—$4.50

FULL EMPLOYMENT, GUIDEPOSTS AND ECONOMIC STABILITY (Third in series of 1966-67 Rational Debates), *Arthur F. Burns* and *Paul A. Samuelson,* 1967—$4.50

THE BALANCE OF PAYMENTS: FREE VERSUS FIXED EXCHANGE RATES (Fourth in series of 1966-67 Rational Debates), *Milton Friedman* and *Robert V. Roosa,* 1967—$4.50

INTERNATIONAL PAYMENTS PROBLEMS (Symposium proceedings, 1966, $7.00)

Papers:

The International Payments System: Postwar Trends and Prospects, *Gottfried Haberler*

Internal Policies Compatible with External Equilibrium at Stable Exchange Rates, *Frederich A. Lutz*

Exchange-Rate Flexibility, *James E. Meade*

The International Payments System: Is There a Shortage of International Liquidity? *Roy L. Reierson*

International Monetary Systems and the Free Market Economy, *Fritz Machlup*

CONGRESS: THE FIRST BRANCH OF GOVERNMENT—1966 ($6.50)

Monographs:

Toward a New Model of Congress, *Alfred de Grazia*

"Check and Balance" Today: What Does It Mean for Congress and Congressmen? *Lewis Anthony Dexter*

Congressional Liaison, *Edward de Grazia*

Introducing Radical Incrementalism into the Budget, *Aaron Wildavsky*

The Committees in a Revitalized Congress, *Heinz Eulau*

Decision Making in Congress, *James A. Robinson*

Legislative Oversight, *Cornelius P. Cotter*

Congress and the Executive: The Race for Representation, *Roger H. Davidson*

The Service Function of the United States Congress, *Kenneth G. Olson*

Availability of Information for Congressional Operations, *Charles R. Dechert*

Information Systems for Congress, *Kenneth Janda*

Strengthening the First Branch: An Inventory of Proposals

Congress: 1989, *Alfred de Grazia*

STUDIES

Federal Grants-in-Aid: Perspectives and Alternatives, *Deil S. Wright*—1968

The Federal Antitrust Laws—Second Revised Edition, *Jerrold G. Van Cise*—1967

Prospects for Reallocating Public Resources. A Study in Federal-State Fiscal Relations, *Murray L. Weidenbaum*—1967

Economic Policy for the Farm Sector, *Hendrik S. Houthakker*—1967

The Swedish Investment Reserve—A Device for Economic Stabilization? *Martin Schnitzer*—1967

Japan: Prospects, Options, and Opportunities, *William J. Sebald* and *C. Nelson Spinks*—1967 ($1.00)

Public Debt in a Democratic Society, *James M. Buchanan* and *Richard E. Wagner*—1967 ($1.00)

Inflation: Its Causes and Cures. With a New Look at Inflation in 1966, *Gottfried Haberler*—1966 ($1.00)

The U.S. Balance of Payments and International Monetary Reserves, *Howard S. Piquet*—1966

The New United Nations—A Reappraisal of United States Policies, *George E. Taylor* and *Ben Cashman*—1965 ($1.00)

French Planning, *Vera Lutz*—1965 ($1.00)

The Free Society, *Clare E. Griffin*—1965, 138 pp. ($4.50)

Congress and the Federal Budget, *Murray L. Weidenbaum* and *John S. Saloma III*—1965, 209 pp. ($4.00)

Poverty: Definition and Perspective, *Rose D. Friedman*—1965 ($1.00)

The Responsible Use of Power: A Critical Analysis of the Congressional Budget Process, *John S. Saloma III*—1964 ($1.00)

Federal Budgeting — The Choice of Government Programs, *Murray L. Weidenbaum*—1964 ($1.00)

The Rural Electrification Administration—An Evaluation, *John D. Garwood* and *W. C. Tuthill*—1963 ($1.00)

The Economic Analysis of Labor Union Power, Revised Edition, *Edward H. Chamberlin*—1963 ($1.00)

United States Aid to Yugoslavia and Poland—Analysis of a Controversy, *Milorad M. Drachkovitch* — 1963 ($1.00)

Communists in Coalition Governments, *Gerhart Niemeyer* — 1963 ($1.00)

Subsidized Food Consumption, *Don Paarlberg*—1963 ($1.00)

Automation—The Impact of Technological Change, *Yale Brozen*—1963 ($1.00)

Essay on Apportionment and Representative Government, *Alfred de Grazia*—1963

American Foreign Aid Doctrines, *Edward C. Banfield*—1963 ($1.00)

The Rescue of the Dollar, *Wilson E. Schmidt*—1963 ($1.00)

The Role of Gold, *Arthur Kemp*—1963 ($1.00)

Pricing Power and "Administrative" Inflation—Concepts, Facts and Policy Implications, *Henry W. Briefs*—1962 ($1.00)

Depreciation Reform and Capital Replacement, *William T. Hogan*—1962 ($1.00)

Consolidated Grants: A Means of Maintaining Fiscal Responsibility, *George C. S. Benson* and *Harold F. McClelland*—1961 ($1.00)

*The Patchwork History of Foreign Aid, *Lorna Morley* and *Felix Morley*—1961 ($1.00)

U.S. Immigration Policy and World Population Problems, *Virgil Salera*—1960 ($1.00)

Voluntary Health Insurance in the United States, *Rita R. Campbell* and *W. Glenn Campbell*—1960 ($1.00)

*United States Aid and Indian Economic Development, *P. T. Bauer*—1959 ($1.00)

Improving National Transportation Policy, *John H. Frederick* — 1959 ($1.00)

The Question of Governmental Oil Import Restrictions, *William H. Peterson*—1959 ($1.00)

Labor Unions and the Concept of Public Service, *Roscoe Pound*—1959 ($1.00)

Labor Unions and Public Policy, *Edward H. Chamberlin, Philip D. Bradley, Gerard D. Reilly,* and *Roscoe Pound*—1958

National Aid to Higher Education, *George C. S. Benson* and *John M. Payne*—1958 ($1.00)

Post-War West Germany and United Kingdom Recovery, *David McCord Wright*—1957 ($1.00)

The Regulation of Natural Gas, *James W. McKie*—1957 ($1.00)

Legal Immunities of Labor Unions, *Roscoe Pound*—1957 ($1.00)

*Involuntary Participation in Unionism, *Philip D. Bradley*—1956 ($1.00)

*The Role of Government in Developing Peaceful Uses of Atomic Energy, *Arthur Kemp*—1956 ($1.00)

*The Role of The Federal Government in Housing, *Paul F. Wendt*—1956 ($1.00)

*The Upper Colorado Reclamation Project. Pro by *Sen. Arthur V. Watkins.* Con by *Raymond Moley*—1956 ($1.00)

---

*Out of print.

LEGISLATIVE AND SPECIAL ANALYSES
90th Congress, Second Session, 1968

Program Priorities in the Budget for Fiscal 1969. *Special Analysis*

Presidential Measures on Balance of Payments Controls. *Special Analysis.* By *Gottfried Haberler* and *Thomas Willett*

Legislative History, 90th Congress, First Session, and Index of AEI Publications

The Debate on Private Pensions

The Debate on Private Pensions. A Condensation of AEI Analysis No. 4. (50 cents)

The Federal Budget for the 1969 Fiscal Year. *Special Analysis*

The Federal Budget for the 1969 Fiscal Year. Statistical Supplement. *Special Analysis*

Proposals for Intermediate Judicial Review of Antitrust Cases

Programs Subject to Spending Reduction Under the Revenue and Expenditure Control Bill

Housing and Urban Development Bills

The "Deceptive Sales" Bill—To Provide for Preliminary Injunctions in Certain Federal Trade Commission Cases

90th Congress, First Session, 1967

*Legislative History, 89th Congress, 2d Session, and Index of AEI Publications ($1.00)

*The Federal Budget for the 1968 Fiscal Year ($1.00)

U.S. Foreign Trade Policy After the "Kennedy Round" ($1.00)

Proposed Social Security Amendments of 1967 ($1.00)

A Convention to Amend the Constitution?—Questions Involved in Calling a Convention Upon Applications by State Legislatures. *Special Analysis* ($1.00)

The "Truth-in-Lending" Bill. Bill by *Sen. Proxmire* ($1.00)

Federal Revenue Sharing Proposals—General Grants to the States with "No Strings Attached" ($1.00)

The President's 1967 Tax Proposals ($1.00)

The Price of the United States Government, 1948-1967. *Special Analysis* ($3.00)

The Proposed National Home Ownership Foundation. Bills by *Sen. Percy; Rep. Widnall* ($1.00)

A Proposed Approach to the Spending Problem. H.R. 10520 by *Rep. Mills* to Create a Commission to Evaluate Federal Programs ($1.00)

Proposals that Deal with National Emergency Strikes ($1.00)

Combating Crime. National High School Debate Series. *Special Analysis* ($1.00)

Should the Federal Government Guarantee a Minimum Cash Income to all Citizens? National College Debate Series. *Special Analysis*

Unless otherwise indicated, all Studies and Analyses—$2.00 per copy.